GOD SPEAKS TO MAN IN

THE END-TIME

ANTHONY A EDDY

Copyright and Publishing

Soft Cover Print ISBN: 978-1-939670-36-6

4. "GOD Speaks to Man in The End-time"

For Searches or Overviews kindly visit www.thewebsiteofthelord.org.nz

	Pages	Content Words
1. GOD Speaks of Return and Bannered	418	87,061
2. GOD Speaks to Man on The Internet	498	122,349
3. GOD Speaks as His Spirit Empowers	272	65,494
4. GOD Speaks to Man in The End-time	166	36,210
5. GOD Speaks in Letters of Eternity	202	45,842
6. GOD Speaks to His Bridal Presence	332	75,373
7. GOD Speaks to His Edifice	514	122,516
8. GOD Speaks of Loving His Creation	280	67,234
9. GOD Speaks Now of a Seal Revealed	124	23,260

Prepared on a 27in iMac™© with the use of Nisus®© Writer Pro. All trademarks™ and intellectual rights remain the property of their respective owners.

GOD Speaks to Man in

On that which has been long designed to benefit man:
to extend The Call of God for the freewill of man;
to reach out into the loving heart of man,
to set in place lasting friendships:
for the immortality of man.

The End-time

And so are the calls emphasized for man,
brought forthwith to his attention,
demanding nothing in return—
except that born of agapé:
the lay-out on the cross.

Anthony A Eddy
(Scribe)

Contents— Order Received

(2, 3, 4 ...) Denotes following items with a similar or same name as earlier ones

Contents— Alphabetical

(2, 3, 4 ...) Denotes following items with a similar or same name as earlier ones

Contents— Category

(2, 3, 4 ...) Denotes following items with a similar or same name as earlier ones

Introduction

These Divine calls mostly consist of Truth Statements intermixed with counselling and are presented for serious contemplation as to their ramifications and how we approach them in the conclusions we may draw. For they are filled with great significance for these present times.

I testify here to one and all that these calls are not of my writing nor instigation. These calls do not stand alone but smoothly build on the preceding ones as if designed as an unfolding story with an establishing foundation. On the original individual documents the scribe has begun each Divine call with the words: 'And I hear The Lord Jesus saying,' "...". It does not appear necessary to have this phrase repetitively introducing each call in this book. Please take it, therefore, as a 'given' as to the stated origin both by testimony and by claim.

The style of the book preserves the scribal comments in italics; while double quotation marks " " denote and enclose text of a Divine origin. British spelling is used for reasons of national culture. Layout simplifies ease of reading and personal study. Each call itself may be accurately searched from within His website. A concordance or a thesaurus has not been used at any stage prior to, during, or after the receiving of these texts. A dictionary (Oxford Concise™) has sometimes been used to comprehend fully, the words of the Divine voice used in expressing His intent. Because the calls have been received via dictation spoken by the Divine voice directly into the mind, the punctuation is subject to human interpretation. Occasionally however, when required for clarity or emphasis, the capitalisation of words, together with the paragraphing, have also been indicated by the Divine. Minor spelling 'typos' are scribal and the punctuation, together with the titles, usually are, but not always. Multiple subject matters sometimes occur in a particular call which precludes the call's naming being entirely appropriate with respect to descriptive accuracy.

Attached to the end of most items is 'My Content Study Aid' inserted at the request of The Lord Jesus to enhance the benefits found in meditating on and understanding the 'Hows' and 'Whys' of the truth statements and His counselling as found herein. If no such Study Aid exists at the end of an item then there are additional Journaling & Notes pages provided in the Appendix. Please remember this is your book to use in the way which best serves your growth within the discipleship of God.

Great care has been taken to ensure scribal accuracy in hearing and transcribing what are now these printed pages of Divinely originated calls. Every word is as received without later omissions, additions, substitutions or edits.

May The Holy Spirit so testify as such to every enquiring soul.

The End-time Surroundings of Man

"The vagaries of the weather speak of interference in the cycling of The Earth,
        speak of variables beyond their controlling bounds,
        speak of infringing on the constants in equations of great complexity.

The vagaries of the weather sees acceleration,
        sees unreliability,
        sees the exposure of the foolishness of man.

The foolishness of man clings to that which should be discarded,
        seeks others to repair that to which he holds the title,
        repeats the mistakes of yesteryear where the painful lessons still
        remain ignored.

The foolishness of man would exert the effort of his hand to uplift a drunken building in
        an attempt to make it stand,
        would accept the presence of the shifting sand,
        would not seek the rock which still withstands,
        would not plan for a recurrence of distress in or upon the land.

Man should not build on the flood plains of The Earth when temporarily forsaken by
        their rivers,
        where the seas encroach upon the shorelines which do not offer sanctuary,
        where the candles of The Lord flame in casting residues from which escape
        is difficult,
        where the land shakes bringing consternation with failure to the activities of man.

My people should not dwell where My word and My counsel caution otherwise.

Man should not dwell where common sense decries a course of action to the sane.

My people have access to My counsel,
        know the presence of My Spirit,
        know the Fatherhood of God,
        know the love of The Son,
        know the giftings of My Spirit:
        yet still they are carried headlong to a cliff as if led by the lemmings of the day;
        yet still they pay no heed to the history of the stage on which they stand;
        yet still they lack the preparation necessary for inclusion as My bride;
        yet still they have not perceived the end-time in the making;
        yet still My sheep do not ponder on the goats within their midst;
        yet still is My word ignored though with nodding heads,
        with lip service that marks no intent to change,
        no intent to prepare,
        no intent to act—
        even in their own self-interest.

- ANTHONY A EDDY (SCRIBE)

For My people of independence carry no weight of heartfelt concern;
no commitment borne within their hearts,
no realization of the horrors which they are about to face.

Woe to those among My people who hold complacency up before their God.

Woe to those among My people who bring procrastination to the table of The Lord.

Woe to those among My people who with years aplenty,
still are not weaned,
still cannot place the armour,
still do not hear the counsel of My Spirit,
still do not know the gifts of My Spirit,
still are not filled with the fullness of My Spirit,
still do not hearken to their taskings,
do not uplift the willing arms of service,
are only known by God for arrivals and departures where
late and early are transposed just so.

Woe to those who care not for commitment;
who care not for their fellowship;
who care not for their promises;
who care not for their lies;
who care not for their safety:
until it becomes too late for repentance under grace.

Woe to those who are strangers to the tithe,
who tender minimal offerings,
who overlook the first fruits of their labours.

Woe to those who seek grace from,
without responsibility to,
The God who died upon a cross for their eternal well-being.

Let the wise encourage action.
Let the wise prepare their rations.
Let the wise foresee the lack of services soon to be.

Let the wise compile the lists of their needs to survive,
to procure,
to set aside so—
from among the multitudes—
My people are prepared for what is soon to come upon them.

In this end-time of preparation for My bride:
the goats will remain the goats,
the goats will attempt to distract My sheep,
the goats will bleat their interruptions,

the goats will come and go without intent to linger longer
than a circling of the sun.

The goats of man will not share the fodder of My sheep;
will not reap at the expense of others;
will not dwell in false colours among the flock of God,
will not share in that from which contributions are withheld.

For soon the goats of man will not cohabit within the flock of God:
as the end-time harvest is brought into the sanctuaries of God.

For there are those with eyes who do not see,
those with ears who do not hear,
those with hands who do not do,
those with feet who do not go,
those with mouths who do not repent,
those with lips who do not witness,
those with gifts who do not use them.

For these are them who look and sound and act like goats within the flock of God.
For these are them who will not stand before the altar of the lamb dressed as for
a wedding.
For these are them who remain as strangers to discipleship where commitment is as
transient as the zephyrs on a summer's day.
For these are them who allow a promise of the record to lie upon the dust at the
discarding of intent.

So as My bride is selected by My Spirit for presentation to The Father,
so as My bride is justified,
so as My bride is sanctified,
so as My bride is pure,
so as My bride is holy,
so as The Son knows the heart of each is true unto the proclamations of each tongue of
every spirit,
so will the call be heard before the gathered throng,
with righteousness established for eternity,
in the presence of The Lamb.

The bride of Christ is about to meet the test of prophecy as it nears fruition,
is in the time frame of fulfilment,
neither leads to a disowning of His sheep nor of His lambs.

The bride of Christ is built on each man's relationship with God:
for as the heart so carries,
so will the reward be made;
for as the soul so testifies,
so will assurances be given;
for as the body bows,

- ANTHONY A EDDY (SCRIBE)

3

so each spirit is uplifted;
for as the tongues confess,
so the beings of creation transition into
the presence of their God."

My Content Study Aid

_____
_____
_____
_____
_____
_____
_____
_____
_____
_____
_____
_____
_____
_____
_____
_____
_____
_____
_____
_____
_____
_____
_____
_____
_____

The End-time Purity of My Bride

"The superintendency of My church on Earth is under My Spirit,

The Holy Spirit,
The Comforter,
The Counsellor of man.

The superintendency of My church in this end-time of the age of My church requires
active supervision,
active testimonies to man,
active presence in My assemblies,
active favour for My saints,
active counsel in the attacks of Satan,
active relationships with the children of God.

The superintendency of My church prior to the presentation to the Father requires
purity from sin,
purity of intent,
purity of belief,
purity of faith,
purity of love,
purity of the tongue.

Idolatry,
in all its many guises devised by man,
pre-empts man from consideration as a candidate for the bride.

So active sin,
so past sin,
so intent to sin:
strikes at,
to disqualify,
the heart of every candidate—
where repentance has left a slate with text which has not been erased.

Sin carried to the table of The Lord is the denial of the cross,
is the denial of The Father's will,
is the denial of what The Lord accomplished in
the reconciliation of man with his God.

The sinning fool,
the sinning goat,
the agnostic without fear,
the atheist without honour,
drink and eat damnation to their soul:
with the cup of The Lord upon their lips;
with the bread of life within their bellies.

- ANTHONY A EDDY (SCRIBE)

For such as these have no dwelling place reserved in Heaven until a commitment of
the heart in faith:
whereupon grace abounds within their lives as the water removes the stains,
the sins,
the grudges,
the hurts—
prevalent within each life to which the cross has assumed
significance with meaning of great relevance.

The partaking of each lamb of innocence is not a party to intent,
does not have a casualness of attitude,
is not at risk before the table of The Lord set
with the fare for saints.

The superintendency of My church on Earth is exemplary and thorough:
has all the vested records for each day of man;
does not neglect the permissiveness of man;
does not overlook infringements considered minor by man;
does not erase a record which requires repentance,
which is linked to others of like content,
which calls for reparation before erasure is complete,
which encounters forgiveness as still outstanding in a
heart of man.

The superintendency of My church is for the benefit of man,
is for the gathering of man,
is for the offering of a destiny with God beyond the
grave of man,
is for the governance of My church while in the age
of grace with faith for
the acceptance of man."

My Content Study Aid

_____

_____

_____

_____

_____

_____

_____

The End-time Lack of Faith

"The end-time storms within the tribulation of man should concern the heart of man—
for the safety of his body,
for the safety of his soul,
for the safety of his walk with God.

The end-time storms witness to the sin of man,
witness to the evilness of Satan,
witness to the authority of God.

The end-time storms witness to the presence of the end-time,
to the season of tribulation,
to what will surely follow.

The end-time storms are not pleasant to endure;
are fraught with danger for man in denial of The God of created life;
are in fulfilment of the word;
are not in danger of repetition;
are current within the age of grace;
are the harbingers of the inheritance of death for the unrepentant faithless soul.

Beware the angel of death as he calls,
as he cauterizes,
to still satanic influence within the heart of man.

Beware the angel of death as he passes over the dwelling places of man.

Beware the angel of death as he hovers with an appointment over the death zones of the
end-time tribulation.

Beware the angel of death as he calls unto an accounting for the sinful record of the
freewill of man.

For as the sin impales the heart,
so grace with faith becomes the sole means of release.

For as sin binds man to an imprisoned destiny,
so repentance gives access to the key of grace.

For as sin embitters the soul of man,
so his spirit becomes captive to the soul of man.

For as the sinful nature establishes in the character of man,
so grace moves beyond the practicality of the reach of man.

For as sin is carried to the grave of man,
so grace is inaccessible:
with the default confirmed as destiny for the iniquitous soul of man."

- ANTHONY A EDDY (SCRIBE)

The End-time of My People

"My people do not seek access to My word,
         do not respond to what is laid before them,
         do not consider fully the effect upon their lives.

My people are about to be beset by the rampaging of the beast,
         are about to encounter a fight for survival,
         are about to suffer pillage,
         are about to suffer looting,
         are about to be molested in their homes,
         are about to be battered by the storms in which will be encountered the satanic
                 souls of man evident as nightmares in their lives.

My people are about to be pursued by the vindictive soul of man,
               the jealous soul of man,
               the selfish soul of man,
               the greedy soul of man,
               the sexual soul of man,
               the hungry soul of man:
in a season which sees the casting off of all restraint as the cities enact out—
                 become—
                 deteriorate into—
the jungles of The Earth where order is deposed;
         where might becomes the right;
         where the will of man is dispensed from the loaded barrel
                 of a gun.

My people should not rush to and fro in disarray,
         should be prepared to stand their ground,
         should have their defences studied and in place,
         should not plan a route filled with obsequiousness,
         should not crave for that which is unattainable,
         should neither be transfixed nor stilled by what presents before them.

My people should not squander time when it is at a premium,
               when reflexes can save a life,
               when God speaks into a void which fills with faith
                 and action,
               when angels are surrounding and where the prayer
                 of faith converts to the witnessing of miracles.

My people may come to the end of their tether,
         may not know how or what to seek,
         may not remember to give thanks for all which they receive,
         may feel as the deserted and downtrodden in their experiences of the day,

may be weary of their mountains,
may be tired of their repeated journeying.

My people may seek their rest when the effort taxes strength,
may fail to man the barricades when stress is to the fore,
may not defend the ramparts of protection from opening attacks,
may retreat to where defence is no longer tenable when boldness would have
won the day,
may prefer to ignore that which they fear is not within their control,
may feel estranged from God when tribulation rules the day.

The people of God dwell within the arms of the loving God,
dwell within the promises made known to His people,
dwell within the inheritance of the family of God,
dwell within the guardianship of angels,
dwell within the security of the flock of The Good Shepherd,
dwell within the preparation for eternal life,
dwell within the promise of The Father,
dwell within the end-time of the advent of The Lord.

My sheep of the new covenant are being called to a new beginning:
for which they should be prepared."

My Content Study Aid

_____
_____
_____
_____
_____
_____
_____
_____
_____
_____
_____
_____
_____
_____
_____

- ANTHONY A EDDY (SCRIBE)

The End-time Survival of My People

"The end-time survival of My people requires a pro-active stance:
    requires updating of positions of mobs upon the streets,
          of gangs intent to raid,
          of weapons to be encountered—
              both by day and by night,
          of proximity of threat,
          of where a sanctuary exists,
       of where safety in numbers should indicate the gathering of My
             people under the mantle of My hosts.

The end-time survival of My people requires access to the necessities of life:
             to shelter of substance,
             to water in sufficient quantity,
             to food for all the intended mouths,
             to clothing of necessity,
             to means of cooking,
        to the need for hygiene so disease is kept at bay.

The end-time survival of My people will depend on their forethought for the placement of
    their stashes compiled to sustain the time of self-dependence:
       as resources are no longer available for selection,
       as fuel becomes a luxury sought by all,
       as the storm brings damage in its wake,
       as the facilities of man are laid waste before his eyes,
       as rescue becomes the need for the immobilized and trapped,
       as first aid becomes the need for the hurt and the wounded,
    as comforting becomes the need for the frightened and the irresolute,
       as estrangement becomes the tableau for the unprepared,
       as direction becomes the need for the unfortunate at a loss to
             comprehend their situation.

The end-time survival of My people requires concentration on the tasks at hand,
    preparation as the key to needs,
    the stocking of the pantries both for sustenance and care,
    the preservation of the items so usage is not impaired,
    the proximity of instruments,
       of tools:
       to ease the way—
       to light the way—
       to find the way.

The end-time survival of My people is of paramount importance,
        is dependent on the end-time faith,

is wise in following My end-time counsel:
in recognizing the storm of Satan to a saint at large,
in taking precautions for preservation when events within surroundings are seen,

are heard,

are felt,

are known,

to be unstable.

Beware of the debris which clutters,
which puts a life at risk,
through the impact of gravity.

The end-time survival of My people is assisted by the time of prayer,
is motivated when in the presence of the practised tongues of Heaven,
is assured by a close relationship with God where a two-way conversation is
not unknown,
is often the norm,
is common to each day.

My saints should pay attention to both the end-time cataclysm of The Earth—
the birth pangs of the coming forth;
plus the intermixing with the end-time cataclysm
of the multitudes of man—
where death and mayhem prevail until complete:
within their season under Heaven.

So My people are not as the abandoned with a fate of little hope—
are not as the flotsam cast upon a foreshore;
are not as the battered by the dismantlers of the homes of man;
are not as the wounded by flying skittles in the skies;
are not as the swamped left by the surging seas;
are not as the huddled found upon the shaking Earth:
as left for dead.

So My people are to be numbered among the survivors of the tribulation of man;
are to be summoned by the trumpet call of the end of age,
are to be there in purity to greet the groom arriving on the clouds of conquest.

So My people,
the sheep of My flock,
the saints of God,
the sons of God,
the temples of My Spirit:
are approaching the end-time of an age,
the end-time of My Spirit's indwelling,
the end-time of the age of grace:
the end-time which beckons to transition unto the throne of God."

- ANTHONY A EDDY (SCRIBE)

The End-time Wherewithal of Man

"The wherewithal of man to attend to his needs is soon to fracture under stress:
                              to witness shortages in nations,
                              to witness failure of the food chain,
                              to witness scarcity abounding,
                              to witness starvation on display—
              as the obesity of the day becomes the scarecrow of the night.

The wherewithal of man succumbs to his willingness to flee,
              succumbs to his ability to flee,
              succumbs to ignorance of where localities are much improved.

The wherewithal of man is ineffectual
        when encountering the stranding of the unprepared,
                      the withdrawal of the enclaves with retreat into security,
                      the internet as it becomes erratic;
        when encountering the refusals and the offers from the secular and the sacred,
                              from the faithless and the faithful,
                              from the graceless and the graceful.

The wherewithal of man may obtain a short respite,
                      may obtain a time for reflection,
                      may prompt to search,
                      may prompt to obtain,
                      may prompt as a squirrel and to hoard,
                      may fail him in his time of need,
                      may dismay him as he views the desolation,
                      may surprise him as he is stopped and searched with robbery as
                                                              the aim.

The wherewithal of man is frittered away when within the mindset of the fool—
                              he who knows the handshake of the devil;
                      is put to good account when within the mindset of the wise—
                              he who knows the handshake of God.

      For such as man will be,
                      so will man experience.
      For such as man lives,
                      so will he be rewarded.
      For such as man aspires,
                      so will he acquire his destiny."

The End-time of The Indwelling of My Spirit

"The end-time of the indwelling of My Spirit signals the end-time of grace,
the end-time of the present age of perseverance,
the end-time of the record keeping,
the end-time of My Spirit's counsel,
the end-time of My Spirit's gifts,
the end-time of the preparation of My bride,
the end-time of the mortality of My bride,
the onset of My kingdom's rule upon The Earth.

The end-time of the indwelling of My Spirit initiates the attaining of the fullness of
My Spirit,
the attaining of the fullness of the
preparation of My people,
the attaining of the fullness of the
body of My bride.

The end-time of the fullness of indwelling of My Spirit signals the fanfare of the trumpet,
the unfurling of the clouds
of conquest,
the setting of the stage for
an appearance.

The end-time of the fullness of indwelling of My Spirit
welcomes The King of kings unto a throne,
welcomes the transition of man into eternity,
welcomes the setting of the springboard for the stars."

My Content Study Aid

_____
_____
_____
_____
_____
_____
_____
_____
_____

The End-time Sanctification

"The end-time sanctification of My saints dawns upon My people.

The end-time sanctifying of My bride approaches the ending of the age:
                              as set for the preparation of My people while grace abounds.

The end-time sanctifying of those still in need of grace are counselled to erase the slates
                                                        of their accounts—
                    the account awaiting repentance before the God of Grace.

For each nightfall in mortality is as the sand within an hourglass;
              so wisdom would counsel the wise to action the wisdom of the day while it is
                                                                  the day—
              so the devil does not rub his hands in glee at the coming of a dawn.

For grace is not fulfilled at the end of day,
              is not fulfilled at the convenience of man,
              is not fulfilled according to a countdown of a timeline.

For as grace exists in the presence of faith,
              so grace is closed at the instant of the advent,
                                        the coming,
                                        the return,
                    of The Lord—
                        when ears can hear in knowledge;
                        when eyes can see in knowledge:
                        when faith becomes supplanted through evidence declared.

On that day will the new and instant faithful,
                              still with inscriptions on their slates,
                                        cry out in despair.

So will the procrastinators of intentions;
              the fence-sitters in their dithering;
              the agnostics in their thoughtlessness:
              pay an eternal price as the records on their slates reserve their places before a throne
                                                                  of judgment.

The end-time sanctifying of My bride results in the absence of impurity by those who
                                                        were impure;
              results in the absence of waywardness as the spirit establishes the captaincy of
                                                        the soul;
              results in the absence of denial as the fulness of My Spirit acknowledges the
                                                        tongues of Heaven—
              those which are enabled to declare the purity required as for My bride:
                              when so found within the temple so prepared.

The end-time sanctifying of My bride is progressive and deliberate,
is active and repentant,
is objective and sincere.

The end-time sanctifying of My bride is frequent and discarding,
is acquiring and frequenting,
is responsive and recalling.

The end-time sanctifying of My bride is omitting and forsaking,
is turning and forgiving,
is loving and accepting.

The end-time sanctifying of My bride is the quest for holiness within the fear of God.

The end-time sanctification of My bride is the presence of the attribute of holiness in
each temple of The Lord.

The end-time sanctities of My bride occur with nightfall when repentance preserves the
purity unto the coming dawn."

My Content Study Aid

_____
_____
_____
_____
_____
_____
_____
_____
_____
_____
_____
_____
_____
_____
_____
_____
_____
_____
_____

The End-time Feeding of The Faithful

"The end-time feeding of the faithful is a task all in itself,
> is a task which needs addressing,
> is a task in need of a solution,
> is a task which My church is there to fulfill.

The end-time feeding of the faithful speaks of a surge in numbers,
> speaks of the shortening days,
> speaks of overcrowding which before was deemed
>> acceptable for the days encountered,
> speaks of teachers of My word discipling on a
>> grander scale,
> speaks of My people reaching out in ministry to My
>> end-time harvest.

The end-time feeding of the faithful is to satisfy with sustenance the spirits and the souls
> of all who seek—
>> by way of explanation,
>> by way of an active query,
>> by way of faith received as My Spirit's gift,
>> by way of the will of God that none should
>>> perish when the heart of man registers
>>> commitment with a longing for the truth.

The end-time feeding of the faithful follows precept upon precept,
> follows such that the reconciliation offered by the loving God is made known
>> to man,
> follows in order man may learn:
>> the way of righteousness;
>> the way of salvation;
>> the way of redemption;
>> the way of My Spirit's presence;
>> the way of converting a body to a temple of the living God;
>> the way back to the presence of the God of man;
>> the way unto eternal life as the destiny of delight;
>> the way of preparation while man is in mortality as a disciple of
>>> The Lord.

The end-time feeding of the faithful leads to two-way communication with The God of
> Abraham as a child of God within a new covenant,
> to a personal relationship with the God of creation,
> to the destiny of choice in which God would have man prepare to dwell:
>> in love,
>> in fellowship,

in wisdom,
in understanding,
in reverence,
in commitment.

The end-time feeding of the faithful accompanies a walk with God;
accompanies discoveries for the soul,
the spirit,
the body of man;
accompanies the end-time development of man so he
may know his God."

My Content Study Aid

_____

_____

_____

_____

_____

_____

_____

_____

_____

_____

_____

_____

_____

_____

_____

_____

_____

_____

_____

_____

_____

- ANTHONY A EDDY (SCRIBE)

The End-time Supplicant of God

"The end-time supplicant enlists the ear of God,
> knows God as a subscriber to his tongues,
> knows God within the realm of his understanding.

The end-time for the supplicant is the season of tribulation,
> the season of answered prayer,
> the season of a growing relationship in depth.

The end-time for the supplicant is of intense divine companionship,
> is of addressing The Father as 'Abba',
>> as 'Daddy',
>> as 'Dad' as if seated at His feet,
>> as if at home within His presence:
> when all pretence is far behind,
> when sin and pride have no entry on a slate,
> when grace receives due favour from The
>> Spirit's presence.

For such as these the loving God greets with the smile of blessing,
> hearkens to a contrite spirit,
> greets afresh an open heart where rancour is unknown.

For such as these is the inheritance of the cross
> with all the implications based on faith,
> with all the commitments based on the new covenant,
> with all the accruals born of grace enacted.

For such as these did The Messiah come,
> did The Messiah linger on the cross,
> did The Messiah put grace into the freewill choice of man,
> did The Father establish the new covenant:
>> the pathway for the reconciliation of God and man.

For such as these does The Spirit indwell a temple in the making,
> does The Spirit counsel,
> does The Spirit welcome for the record.

For such as these,
> with their temples fully washed and operational,
> can The Spirit come in fullness bringing the promise of The Father.

For such as these will the end-time become the lead-in to the stars.

For such as these will the end-time be welcomed,
> will the end-time be understood,
> will the end-time be seen as the choke-point to the multitudes.

The end-time supplicant of God with commitment embedded in his heart,
embedded in his tongue,
embedded in his soul:
carries his assuredness of entry to his destiny—
as he has so persevered."

My Content Study Aid

_____

_____

_____

_____

_____

_____

_____

_____

_____

_____

_____

_____

_____

_____

_____

_____

_____

_____

_____

_____

_____

_____

_____

_____

_____

_____

_____

_____

The End-time Coming of The Lord

"The end-time coming of The Lord is a once-off event of impact
for the multitudes of The Earth,
for all those waiting in expectation,
for all those with hearts of scepticism,
for all those surprised who lived within denial
of all they now hear and see.

The end-time coming of The Lord follows the season of the tribulation—
that so named by man which trivializes what is to
build into a climax which will shake The Earth,
which is to fragment the constructions of man,
which is to wipe from the face of The Earth the enclaves
of iniquity where man practises what he will;
the season of the end-time trial of My saints where betrayal is the norm,
where justice is not evident,
where the calls for help fall on deafened ears,
where the needs of life no longer are on sale—
are plundered within the will of man;
the season both of death and of destruction falling on the unprepared,
falling on the wicked with the wrath of God displayed,
falling on the saints of God according to their preparation,
according to their understanding,
according to the prayer lives of the saints.

The end-time coming of The Lord signs the end of grace,
signs the introduction of a new era where time is absent,
where the clock of man is
discarded with
his mortality,
where the events of movement
have new parameters
of control;
signs the transitioning of the body of man into the similitude of the
body of The Christ of Advent,
signs the transitioning of The Earth into The Earth reborn from the
impurities instated by and
during the mortality of man,
into The Earth fit for the presence of the Kingdom of
God in its fullness,
into The Earth where satanic influence is restricted by
imprisonment for an age of reigning
righteousness before the throne of God,

into The Earth where man is to experience justice mixed
with mercy—
from the throne and from the seat—
as the multitudes so gather with the tasks of allocation,
where ageing is now present only as a memory,
where tears of mourning no longer wet the cheeks of man,
where opportunity and advancement no longer cause the striving of
the soul,
where the human spirit dwells in safety and security within the
family of God,
where the citizens of His kingdom know the enduring benevolence
of The Loving Living God—
as He attends His bride—
as His bride attends Him."

My Content Study Aid

_____

_____

_____

_____

_____

_____

_____

_____

_____

_____

_____

_____

_____

_____

_____

_____

_____

_____

_____

The End-time of Consumption

"The end-time of consumption will see scarcities appear in the supplies of man,
     will see insufficiencies arise for the demands of man,
     will see the empty shelves which mark the unwillingness
         to supply at the prices so requested,
     will see the food chains of The Earth under stress to
          surmount the interruptions
          brought by man,
     will see the necessities of life being bid for at the market
          place in exchange for gold,
     will see the loss of trust as nations with their paper
          promises lose value not inherent
          in their modicums of exchange.

The end-time of consumption will encounter difficulties
       in obtaining a replacement guarantee,
       in obtaining stable pricing,
       in obtaining access to a surplus placed on offer.

The end-time of consumption will stretch the purses of man,
     will stretch the rationing to man,
     will stretch the accounts of man with the money-lenders of
         the day,
     will stretch a mirthless grin across a face as credit sought is
         met with a blank refusal,
     will stretch the promises received until they fracture
         without honouring
         upon a broken pile,
     will stretch the gullibility of man past what should be the
         limits of his common sense.

The end-time of consumption changes the values placed upon commodities,
     discards the values of the past as of little relevance,
     brings the values attributed to the expectations of
         the morrow,
    uses the values which contribute to,
      which will encourage,
     an on-going supply in the face of profits being
     garnished from the shortage of materials,
       the shortage of transportation,
       the shortage of production,
       the shortage of supply brought through the
         suddenly-selfish in terms of
         food production,

the shortage of irrigation brought through the
changing pattern of the water
distribution on The Earth,
the shortage of the energy required for
completion of the contracts detailing
the trading commerce of man.

The end-time of consumption is affected by the environment of the end-time—
of wars,
of storms,
of pestilence,
of droughts,
of floods,
of inhospitable weather patterns befalling the ill-informed,
of stockpiling by the nations;
by the cartels of monopolies;
by the chains of commerce sourcing from distant lands;
by the machinations of man;
of the suffering,
of the starvation,
of the death:
resulting from the freewill of man which exhibits either greed or the lack
of preparation—
the absence of foresight—
the misunderstanding of what is soon to be encountered—
the ignoring of the seriousness of the warnings and the signs—
those which speak of the onset of the end-times with all which that entails."

My Content Study Aid

_____

_____

_____

_____

_____

_____

_____

_____

_____

_____

_____

The End-time of Collisions

"The end-time of collisions records the clashes of the will of man with the will of man,
    inherits the clashes of the will of Satan with the will of man,
    suffers the clashes of the will of man with the will of God.

The end-time of collisions speaks of the circling and the approaches,
                of the charges and the defeats,
                of the offers and the acceptances,
                of the rejections and the destruction,
                of the savagery and the deaths,
                of the fear and the consolation.

The end-time of collisions speaks of the addictions and the diseases,
                of the maladies and the pain,
                of the afflictions and the causes,
                of the sinning and the encouraging.

The end-time of collisions speaks of the pig-headedness and the determination,
                of the secular and the sacred,
                of the guilty and the innocent,
                of the wayward and the forgiving,
                of the lost and the saved,
                of the careless and the careful,
                of the impatient and the patient,
                of the mortal and the eternal.

The end-time of collisions indicates the heart-intent of man,
                indicates the seal to be selected for imprinting upon a life,
                indicates the destination likely for a soul;
                confirms the records of the angels,
                confirms a blank page in a book where the entry has not
                                been sought,
                confirms a soul who over-rides the preferences of the spirit
                                while the body is still mortal.

The end-time of collisions resounds the praises of God to those gathered in His flock,
                to those-in-waiting for a
                                special day,
                to those who understand the
                                season which befalls,
                to those preparing for a wedding
                                of exceptional renown.

For such as these dwell under the extended right arm of God;
                the promise of The Father;

the new covenant of The Son;
the counsel of The Spirit:
in this age of grace.

For such as these dwell in the household of faith,
in the inheritance of promise,
in the light of Christ revealed unto the world.

For such as these are covered by the mantles of:
the promise to those martyred;
the promise inherent in the body and the blood;
the promise released for the committed from the
death upon the cross;
the promise of the coming of The Risen King."

My Content Study Aid

_____

_____

_____

_____

_____

_____

_____

_____

_____

_____

_____

_____

_____

_____

_____

_____

_____

_____

_____

_____

_____

- ANTHONY A EDDY (SCRIBE)

The End-time Conflicts of Man

"The end-time conflicts of man often will express the savagery within the soul of man,
    often will arise in man's attempt to conquer,
            to dominate,
            to exact vengeance for what has gone before;
    often will result from perceptions built on envy,
            on greed,
            on self-aggrandizement,
            on the grab for land at a time of an
                  opponent's weakness;
    often will declare an ultimatum noted for its unacceptability,
    often will provoke a sneak attack built upon deceit,
    often will promote the pillaging of the needs of others without regard to life.

The end-time conflicts of man counsel and condone the weapons mixed with violence,
        the battering rams of intrusion with destruction,
        the arson of the homes with incineration of all hope,
        the shells exploding the poisons of man via the timing fuses,
        the bomb-blasts from the heavens aimed to lay waste the villages with
                the lives of innocents,
        the atrocities rendered to the cities with the pitted bloodstained walls—
              which rise from the huddled forms.

The end-time conflicts of man erase each cynosure from the eyes of man,
           replace such with the rubble of the age,
           seek the supremacy of the beast,
           greet the obstacles with excessive force,
           proceed within the darkness of the night,
           dispense the building blocks of hatred to frequent
                the generations.

The end-time conflicts of man do not last indefinitely,
           are as a blotch upon the face of man
         where mercy can be seen as non-existent;
         where determination melts into exhaustion;
         where disfigurements should show as badges of dishonour;
         where the eyes of the soul reflect only an inward Hell;
         where the germs of war fester with the seeking of dominion;
         where there is no right to be except among the death throes
                of a people,
                of a nation,
                of a tongue;
         where the segments of the multitudes of man so consign
             themselves for destruction—

at each other's hands under satanic instruction—
as their ears become immune to the call of God.

The end-time conflicts of man gather into the storm of man,
are thrust before the face of God,
are filled with the blasphemy of man,
are solidified by the lies of man,
are superimposed upon the vision of the damned,
are visible as the cohorts of the devil,
are led as by the rider of the red horse—
are those who see the pale horse,
with its rider,
unleashed to wander within the boundaries as set—
to tread the conflicts of man—
to bring the reign of death to man.

The end-time conflicts of man result in the dead unburied,
result in the sounding of the death knell for the combatants,
result in the ravaging of the body by the viruses of the soul,
result in the lost encountering the first and second death.

The end-time conflicts of man are unaware of the coming change in ownership of that for
which the battles rage—
the lands and the interests of man.

The end-time conflicts of man do not serve the cause of justice,
do not serve the instilling of righteousness,
do not place peace before the malcontents,
do not own the right to vengeance as evidenced by the acts
of man.

The end-time conflicts of man vary in extension,
vary in ferocity,
vary on the fields of slaughter,
vary in the flaring of disputes,
vary in the waging of the wars of man,
vary in the leadership and the objectives of the villains
seeking gain.

So the innocent are trampled to be left out of breath.

So the saints of God are martyred under threat.

So The Earth is in the season of preparation for the bride of Christ."

- ANTHONY A EDDY (SCRIBE)

The End-time Excessive Wealth of Man

"The end-time of the success of man in compiling wealth beyond his needs is of witness
in itself—
as fortunes vaporize as if held within a fog bank in the dawn,
are lost upon the sun rise of the fraud,
are not reborn upon the appearance of the dusk.

The end-time excessive wealth of man gained without a purpose dissipates
as jelly on a road baking in the sunlight,
as water through a sieve without a pail,
as water on a sandy shore without
a scoop,
as when washed without a screen in a
raging torrent which
carries all before.

The end-time excessive wealth of man speaks of how it is obtained by overcharging,
how it is generated by foolish valuations,
how it is condoned by the gearing wheels
which multiply,
how it is found hidden for discovery,
how it is created in the networks of ones and zeroes,
how it is frittered from a game of chance.

The end-time excessive wealth of man speaks of how it is interred in the vaults
of darkness:
as if marooned from the life of the sun.

The end-time excessive wealth of man is only rarely earned,
is only rarely justified,
is only rarely knighted by a blessing.

The end-time excessive wealth of man often demonstrates commonality in accumulation,
often demonstrates commonality in dispersal.

The end-time excessive wealth of man can come and go without appreciation for
opportunities not realized,
not taken-up,
not foreseen in wisdom for what they really are.

The end-time excessive wealth of man can damage reputations in its accrual,
can bring the honouring of man in its allocations
to the cause of merit.

The end-time excessive wealth encountered by man
is a challenge in disposal where happiness is the goal of life,

is a challenge in sharing where many hands are opened,
is a challenge in keeping where the soul becomes endangered,
is a challenge before the courts of man where fragmentation is the goal,
is a challenge from with-holding where justice is not served,
is a challenge to success where guarding becomes the prime objective.

The end-time excessive wealth is handled correctly by the walk of righteousness,
by the heart which seeks the light of truth,
by the soul which knows its destiny through choice,
by that character of man which acknowledges the
powers of good and evil:
and can perceive the value in the difference."

My Content Study Aid

_____
_____
_____
_____
_____
_____
_____
_____
_____
_____
_____
_____
_____
_____
_____
_____
_____
_____
_____
_____
_____

- ANTHONY A EDDY (SCRIBE)

The End-time of Deceit

"The end-time of deceit is about to grow and prosper,
    is soon to introduce the knaves of The Earth,
    is to introduce the real meaning of ill-gotten gain.

The end-time of deceit is spreading across The Earth,
    is found in every pocket without accountability,
    is widespread in its application,
   reaches out across all valued aspects of the life of man.

The end-time of deceit attacks the integrity of man,
    shrinks the pools of honesty,
    expands the seas of lies:
      the bedrock of deceit;
      the breeding place of fraud;
  the nesting place which harbours the birthplace of the schemes,
     which encourages the low road to acquisition,
     which circumvents the working hands of man,
     which summarizes for belief that later seen as not so,
     which searches among the temptations of the soul,
     which locks in the weakened spirit so the soul may acquiesce.

 Beware the nests which raise the hatchlings which squawk out for attention,
    which persevere well past the declining of an offer,
    which will seek repeating contributions from the greedy,
        from the gullible,
        from the naive of station and of life.

The end-time of deceit sees deception to the fore—
     with a plausible excuse—
 ready for a query as to the specifics of intent:
    as the knock falls upon a door,
    as an eMail is delivered,
    as a stamp is placed upon an envelope,
    as the telephone brings a call at mealtimes,
    as an 'Excuse me' in the street,
    as a hand outreached in preparation with a begging bowl,
    as a contract is presented for a signature in ignorance,
    as documents bequeathing access are sought without the validation.

The end-time of deceit flourishes in the season of high activity,
     in the presence of a change of scene,
     in the unfamiliarity with new protocols of direction,
     in the chasing after opportunities,
     in the acceptance of what appears with a menu of free lunch,

in the lack of checks and balances performed,
in the loss of common sense at the unfolding of the story,
in the absence of sought counsel from the wise.

The end-time of deceit festers on the misplaced trust,
on the acquaintance rated as a friend,
on the urgency associated with acceptance,
on the guise of the availability of wealth where acumen
is untested,
on the possession of means left unverified,
on the record of behaviour remaining obscured,
on the remoteness of the transfer precluding a recovery,
on the details of the information being hidden as in a cellar
without a light or key.

Beware of the initial surge of the hope,
of the expectation,
of the promised change in circumstance,
of the references at distance,
of the loan,
of the fee,
of the deposit,
of the gift,
of the funding transfer,
of the loaded card of commerce:
those sought in preparation of the promised scheme—
which has no payday in reality,
which feeds on finding willing victims,
which is effective in denuding such of their nest eggs—
for transfer to another hidden nest."

My Content Study Aid

_____
_____
_____
_____
_____
_____
_____
_____
_____

The End-time Events of Man

"The end-time events of man are muddled in their formats,
        are muddled in their impact,
        are muddled in their exhortations,
        are muddled with perceptions,
        are muddled with the implications,
        are muddled with the expectations.

The end-time events of man come and go at the freewill of man;
       reflect the ignobility of the end-time freewill of man,
       reflect the barbarity of the hidden soul of man,
       reflect the avarice of the end-time character of man,
       reflect the estrangement of the spirit of man from The Spirit
                  of The Living God.

The end-time events of man have their sourcing from the heavens,
       have their sequencing from the heavens,
       have their prophesying from the heavens.

The end-time events of man have the choreography arising from the heavens with an
            allocation to the freewill of man,
       to the season for the playwrights to present the deeds
          envisaged upon the end-time stage,
       to the denoting of the finale of the symphony of grace.

The end-time events of man have satanic overtones,
       have demonic underscores,
       have the spells of witches,
       have the curses of the idolaters down through the ages,
       have the frenzies of the insane surfacing in fantasies,
       have the spectacle of the mashing of the blending of the
        heartless guile with and of the spooking of the villains—
         placing no emphasis either on truth or reliability—
        as they cheer in their pursuance of the destruction of
          integrity when demons exercise control.

The end-time events of man will come as a surprise to man,
       will come with a lack of understanding,
       will come with the multitudes filled with unbelief,
       will come upon the unprepared,
       will come upon the ill-advised,
       will come upon the unprotected.

The end-time events of man are suffered unto death,
       are experienced unto extermination,

are witnessed by the slaughtering of man,
are party to dismembering,
are present at disembowelling,
are subject to great torture.

The end-time events of man call forth the confessions of man;
call forth the betrayals of man;
call forth the lies of man;
call forth the threats,
the onset,
of excruciating pain;
call forth the false promises of survival;
call forth the deaths of agony.

The end-time events of man call forth the deceptions of man birthed to supplement his
freewill desire,
call forth the instruments of torture,
call forth the death masks on the countenances of man,
call forth the stench of death,
call forth the rotting of the flesh,
call forth the picking of the bones.

The end-time events of man preclude the counting of the dead,
preclude the burying of the dead,
preclude the hearts with mercy from a presence
within the spreading of the pestilence,
within the fields of fire,
within the ministries of the angels
from the throne room.

The end-time events of man preclude the hearts of mercy from attending to the needs of
man who willingly participates.

The end-time events of man address an epic struggle,
address the evil accumulated on The Earth,
address the cleansing necessary prior to the rebirth,
prior to the new beginning,
prior to the transitioning of
man to a steady state.

The end-time events of man sear the memories of survival,
sear the memories of the scenes,
sear the memories of actions carried out within mortality,
sear the records which are closed,
sear the records remaining open,
sear the eyes of God through the presence of The Holy Spirit,
sear The Lamb's Book of Life with the finality of the seal of
life within mortality."

- ANTHONY A EDDY (SCRIBE)

The End-time Speaks

"The end-time speaks,
      within its season,
            of the maturing of the environment of man;
            of the religiosity of man;
            of the deviant faiths of man,
            of the opening of the sword of My Spirit as it cuts and thrusts with the
                                  fulfilment of the prophecies,
                      as it lays bare the showcase of
                            the truth:
          implicit through the ages of man in the living loving God declared,
                              proclaimed,
                              foretold,
                              presented,
                              witnessed,
                              sacrificed,
                              testified:
         for the understanding acceptance of man in need of reconciliation when
                grace is to the fore in the presence of freewill.

The end-time speaks with many voices,
          with many topics of dependence:
          with much foolishness,
          with much wisdom,
          with much thought,
          with much consideration:
       for that which is soon to come to pass before the eyes of man's mortality.

The end-time speaks across The Earth,
          across the seas,
          across the heavens of The Earth:
                of a startling change in circumstances,
                of amazing enticements of man,
                of many falls from favour,
                of many depredations of man on man,
                of the scouring of the landscapes for a morsel for the mouth,
                of the seeking of a place where trust and truth are honoured.

The end-time speaks in closure with events of grandeur associated with a King,
                with a King in waiting,
                with a King in prophesy,
                with a King of great authority,
                with a King with consummate power,
                with a King of retinue,

with a King as unto a Kingdom,
with a King who shall not be dispossessed,
with a King who heralds the aeons of the present.

The end-time speaks of much loss of life,
of much mourning for the damned,
of much martyring of the saints,
of much celebrating by the saved,
of much enquiring from the lost—
as seeking speaks to hearts where faith is being kindled from a
spark of knowledge.

The end-time speaks of great expectations,
of the fulfilment of the destinies of man,
of the achieving of a major milestone in the grand design of God,
of the proximity of the rebirths as promised,
of the spotlessness of a pristine environment,
of the crossing of the finish line in the race of life within mortality,
of the transference of the goal with eyes set on eternity,
of the transitioning of being into the presence of the God of Love,
of the inheritance in its fullness disclosed unto His saints."

My Content Study Aid

_____
_____
_____
_____
_____
_____
_____
_____
_____
_____
_____
_____
_____
_____
_____

- ANTHONY A EDDY (SCRIBE)

The End-time Website of The Lord

"The website of The Lord is due for a change in emphasis;
for a freeing from the law of recompense while
in preparation;
for the instating of the freewill offerings of faith:
while man is under grace,
as fullness is attained,
so the good news is proclaimed.

The website of The Lord reaches out in disclosure,
fulfils The Spirit's guidance,
knows the evidence of truth.

The website of The Lord links the past into the future,
links the present to understanding,
links the destiny of man unto his own freewill,
links the curses with their origins,
links the blessings to the reign,
links wisdom to requests so wisdom may prevail.

The website of The Lord places emphasis on knowledge of The God of Love,
places emphasis on preparation,
places emphasis on the opened door,
places emphasis on knowledge of the season,
places emphasis on the divine relationship,
places emphasis on the selecting of a destiny,
places emphasis on enquiry with response,
places emphasis on the immortality of man.

The website of The Lord stands to introduce man to his God,
to strengthen a divine relationship through knowledge of
the day,
to bring again the love of God before the attention of man.

The website of The Lord does not succumb to evil,
does not honour man in his own sight,
does not condone sin in all its forms.

The website of The Lord would motivate man in righteousness:
to forsake his pride,
to maintain integrity of character,
to subdue his soul unto his spirit,
to welcome his destiny of choice,
to grow into discipleship,
to leave the goats behind,

to decide to join the shepherd in
the sheepfold:
in the coming reign of light.

The website of The Lord shouts the message of salvation to a hungry world,
to encourage those born to seek,
to witness departures from idolatry,
to be at the forefront of acceptance at
the rejoicing of the angels,
to discover the need for knowledge of
The Living God,
to fill the mind of man
with the message of the cross,
with the reality of redemption,
with the planning for eternity in the
presence of The God of Grace."

My Content Study Aid

_____

_____

_____

_____

_____

_____

_____

_____

_____

_____

_____

_____

_____

_____

_____

_____

_____

_____

_____

- ANTHONY A EDDY (SCRIBE)

The End-time of Consensus

"The end-time of consensus is about to be consigned to history.

The end-time of consensus will prove to be unworkable,
                    will prove to have outlived its functioning,
                    will prove to be incompatible with that which is expected.

The end-time of consensus will see democracy retired,
        will see governments of man forsake the causes of dissent,
        will see the abandonment of religious persecution after
                          the tribulation,
        will see the inauguration of Kingdom rule upon The Earth
                with the instatement of The Father's will,
      as the prayer of discipleship is answered,
      as The Son returns to reign in righteousness and peace
          with the blessing of The Father and the
          gathering of the bride.

The end-time of consensus will see the removal of the plotters,
        the removal of the militarists,
          the removal by destruction of the misfiring weapons
               so pointed at man,
       the removal of the power bases born of greed
              and cunning.

The end-time of consensus will not serve the mighty with overloaded prisons,
        will not serve conglomerates where mercy is unknown,
        will not serve cartels where pricing is sustained through
             competition under threat.

The end-time of consensus will not serve the men of yesterday who would preserve the
               status quo,
        will not serve the games of chance with
               predetermined outcomes,
        will not serve the managed storehouses where price is
           the release,
        will not serve the selfishness of man that seeks to spread
          the blame.

The end-time of consensus will not subdue the life of tyrants,
        will not confront those ignoring the call of hunger,
        will not address injustice hidden under other names,
        will not re-offer that which has been emptied of its value,
        will not retreat against a wave of protest,
        will not preserve the happiness of man."

The End-time of Recalibration

"The end-time of recalibration approaches the timing of relief,
>experiences the freedom from correction,
>knows the certainty of positioning,
>the certainty of travelling,
>the certainty of the events of life when the clock of
>man is no longer relevant,
>is no longer needed,
>is no longer the governor of all life
>>on Earth.

The end-time of recalibration bespeaks the loss of livelihoods,
>bespeaks the loss of reference,
>bespeaks the loss of relativity as the lynchpin is removed.

The end-time of recalibration frees the spirit,
>the soul,
>the body of man
>from the subjugation of masterful control,
>from the imperiousness of a passing sequence,
>from the imperviousness of interference from the intellect of man,
>from the pre-emption of the lack of choice available to man.

The end-time of recalibration bemoans the extent of change,
>bemoans the losing of position,
>bemoans the forsaking of a history,
>bemoans the measurement accompanying man in
>>his mortality,
>bemoans the running down of the ticking of the metronome
>as it accompanies,
>>in a duet of death,
>>the sand within the hourglass of man.

The end-time of recalibration speaks of new things in the pipeline bringing a new
>>approach to life:
>speaks of the need for understanding,
>speaks of the need for preparation,
>speaks of the call of angels,
>speaks of the call of man,
>speaks of the curtain call for grace.

The end-time of recalibration speaks to the prophecies of The Living God laid before the
>>face of man,
>to the prophecies with independence from the
>timetabling of man,

- ANTHONY A EDDY (SCRIBE)

to the prophecies of illumination laid for the discernment
of man,
to the prophecies of present truth spread upon the table
of The Lord for the encouragement of man,
to the prophecies of impact on man in his environment
declared for the on-going benefit of man,
to the prophecies of the wrath of God falling on man for
the destruction of carried sin when still
found within the heart of man.

The end-time of recalibration speaks for the prepared of God,
speaks for the sheep within the sheepfold,
speaks for the bride of Christ with purity attained,
speaks for the termination of the age of grace,
speaks for The Loving God who waits with His arms
outstretched to welcome."

My Content Study Aid

_____

_____

_____

_____

_____

_____

_____

_____

_____

_____

_____

_____

_____

_____

_____

_____

_____

_____

_____

The End-time Experience of Tribulation

"The end-time experience of tribulation is a sequence of fast-moving events,
is a panorama of The Earth spinning to
man's destruction,
is of freewill gone berserk,
is of demonic activity without adequate control,
is of the wrath of God spent on the ungodly.

The end-time experience of tribulation unfastens and releases,
unyokes and dispenses,
unsettles and dismisses.

The end-time experience of tribulation carves up the meal of separation,
serves up the dessert of portions,
clears the table of the scraps not fit for dogs.

The end-time experience of tribulation looses the presence of the shrunken stomach,
binds the fountain from cascading,
ignores the rivers of water filled with life.

The end-time experience of tribulation causes man to stumble in the heat,
brings man to shiver in the cold,
leads man to lean into the wind.

The end-time experience of tribulation reverses the environment of man:
brings darkness where once was light,
brings violence where once was harmony,
brings chaos where once was structure,
brings anarchy where once was rule,
brings starvation where once was food,
brings deceit where once was trust.

The end-time experience of tribulation sights the laying bare of signed death warrants as
foreclosed in time—
as a week of both nights and days totals each fresh witness to
ten thousand times ten thousand spread out upon The Earth—
to fuel the fires of acrimony,
to stoke the fires of vengeance,
to sear the souls of the damned:
those who never sought the freeing of
the body,
soul and spirit.

The end-time experience of tribulation marks the revelatory point in the reality of the
relationship between man and God.

- ANTHONY A EDDY (SCRIBE)

The end-time experience of tribulation closes to vistas long awaited by the sheep,
　　　　　　　　　to preparations long requested through
　　　　　　　　　　　　prophetic declarations,
　　　　　　　　　to events unfolding from the throne room
　　　　　　　　　　　　　　of God,
　　　　　　　　　to visits of enactment before the face
　　　　　　　　　　　　　　of man,
　　　　　　　　　to the priceless with the precious seen
　　　　　　　　　　　advancing with the touchstone for
　　　　　　　　　　　eternal destinies."

My Content Study Aid

_____

_____

_____

_____

_____

_____

_____

_____

_____

_____

_____

_____

_____

_____

_____

_____

_____

_____

The End-time of Complaint

"The end-time of complaint is soon to beset The Earth,
        is soon to be heard both wide and far,
        is soon to fill the ears of man with the babble of the nations,
          of the peoples,
          of the tongues of the multitudes—
    those who have no interest in The God who calls His sheep by name.

The end-time of complaint darkens the outlook of man,
        hearkens to the call of Satan,
        makes hoarse the voice of man in the ears of God.

The end-time of complaint speaks of little worth the listening,
        speaks of little worth the harbouring,
        speaks of little worth allocating to the memory of man.

The end-time of complaint visits the like-minded,
        visits the surly,
        visits the unforgiving.

The end-time of complaint builds a fabric frayed around the edges,
        a fabric full of holes,
        a fabric where the worms are comfortably at home,
        a fabric never washed by blood,
        a fabric of impurity from where truth has long
            since flown.

The end-time of complaint does not seek solutions,
        does not listen to wise counsel,
        does not give up gnawing on a rotten bone.

The end-time of complaint drags down the ears of man,
        mimics the mumbling of man as an audience is sought,
        blisters the tongue of man from excessive repetition.

The end-time of complaint brings the destruction of the value in concern,
        of the concern in value.

The end-time of complaint scores little with the busy,
        scores little with the bouyant:
        scores little in the progress of the stakes of interest to the soul.

The end-time of complaint weakens the helpful with the burdens born of selfishness,
        overlooks revealing all the points of relevancy,
        disparages the views formed from good intent,
        sings a song of misery causing departure of the listening ears.

- ANTHONY A EDDY (SCRIBE)

The end-time of complaint collaborates with evil in the targeting of man:
collaborates with evil to pull down the edifice of God
on Earth;
collaborates with evil to construct a framework of despair in
the heart of man;
collaborates with evil to prevent thereby the return of man
back into the presence of The Eternal God of life.

The end-time of complaint bands together all those
who will be seized in fire—
unless there is a record of an act
signifying a change of heart;
who will scream in the emptiness of darkness—
unless there is a record of repentance;
who will be held imprisoned by the binding chains—
unless there is a record of commitment
to Jesus,
The Living Christ,
while in this age of grace."

My Content Study Aid

_____
_____
_____
_____
_____
_____
_____
_____
_____
_____
_____
_____
_____
_____
_____
_____

Thankful are The Poor in Spirit

"Thankful are the poor in spirit as their spirits attempt to navigate their souls,
    as their spirits learn to soar,
    as their spirits hear the claps of angels with messages for
      the souls in need of the vitality of life.

Thankful are the poor in spirit as they rest to overcome,
    as they rest within a sanctuary,
    as they rest upon the word.

Thankful are the poor in spirit as they thirst for discipleship,
    as they thirst for an inheritance,
    as they thirst beside a brook of flowing water which leads
      to the river of the waters of life—
      where they no longer suffer thirst.

Thankful are the poor in spirit found rejoicing in the wealth of their souls,
    found rejoicing in the dances gifted to their spirits,
    found rejoicing at the goodness of their God.

Thankful are the poor in spirit with their countenances filled with smiles,
    with their tongues of praise way above a murmur,
    with the counsel of My Spirit studied phrase by phrase.

Thankful are the poor in spirit as they seek to acquire a stable walk with God,
    as they scramble as a student before the wisdom of
      the universe,
    as they acknowledge by their postures the holiness of God.

Thankful are the poor in spirit for the knowledge of their God,
    for the presence of My Spirit trailing gifts,
    for the glory of the sunbeams bringing sparkling to
      the eyes,
    for the seizing of the moment to commune with God,
    for the enrichment of their fellows as they too find the
      river flowing,
    for the grace of God's anointing with forgiveness as it
      restores each soul from sin.

Thankful are the poor in spirit for they know full well where they stand,
    know full well the trials of life,
know full well the vicissitudes encroaching on each day,
know full well the handiwork of God with the offered hand in welcome,
know full well the significance bestowed upon a change of heart,
know full well the impact of the loving God upon the lives of those in need."

- ANTHONY A EDDY (SCRIBE)

The Fragrance of My Spirit (2)

"The fragrance of My Spirit awakes the world to wonder,
>> awakes the world to discernment,
>> awakes the world to attempt to see the source.

The fragrance of My Spirit does not linger past The Son-rise,
>> does not frequent the vapours of the swamp,
>> does not disturb the comfort of the lost in their days
>>>> of reflection.

The fragrance of My Spirit is the sign of The Presence,
>> is a sign of confirmation,
>> is a sign that all is well within the soul,
>> is a sign unto the spirit that guards both day and night,
>> is a sign that grace is granted with the slate erased.

The fragrance of My Spirit comes at a time of rest,
>> comes at a time of waiting,
>> comes at a time when holiness opens the temple of The Lord.

The fragrance of My Spirit rewards a seeking spirit,
>> rewards an open heart,
>> rewards a servant held in trust.

The fragrance of My Spirit removes the odours of the world,
>> removes the stains upon a gown,
>> confirms the validity of an entered record of The Son.

The fragrance of My Spirit glides silently in approach,
>> passes a message of the love of God unto the nostrils of man,
>> touches the three-in-one entity of man with the peace of God.

The fragrance of My Spirit attends at the will of God,
>> attends the peaceful and the reconciled,
>> attends the temples of the family of God.

The fragrance of My Spirit is an outward sign to man of the status of his inner being,
>> is an outward sign to man which binds him in the bonds
>>>> of love,
>> is an outward sign to man of the welcome extended by his
>>>> presence to The Spirit of The Living God.

The fragrance of My Spirit is to be recognized and honoured,
>> is to be appreciated with all due fear,
>> is to be welcomed with gratitude so the temple may be
>>>> extended into a living space of grandeur.

The fragrance of My Spirit attends the growth of man,
> attends in teaching the majesty and the glory available
>> through faith,
> attends the confirmation of man as he is capped with his
>> degree from the university of the mortality of man.

The fragrance of My Spirit attends the rejoicing graduation of man as man moves into the
> presence of his God."

Scribal Note:
> *Refer also to* 'The Fragrance of The Spirit' *in His 2nd book—*
> 'God Speaks to Man on The Internet'
>> *freely available and searchable on* The Website of The Lord.

My Content Study Aid

_____

_____

_____

_____

_____

_____

_____

_____

_____

_____

_____

_____

_____

_____

_____

_____

_____

_____

_____

_____

_____

_____

The Beauty of The Morning

"The beauty of the morning is often not seen regularly by man,
                not seen when playing to an empty house,
                not seen as the curtain rises as the menu of the day.

The beauty of the morning is clothed in glory with the sun-rise,
             is clothed in regality with the earth-light lingering in the dawn,
             is clothed in majesty with the clouds displayed on fire.

The beauty of the morning showcases the tail-end of the dressings of the night,
             showcases the presenting of the day,
             showcases the pattering of The Earth in season,
             showcases the mantling of white as the backdrop changes,
             showcases the impact of a shoreline plashing a
                              bounded beach,
             showcases the foresting of the trees intersected by the streams
                                of purity.

The beauty of the morning succumbs to the lighting of the day,
             succumbs to the headlight of The Son,
             succumbs to the passage of the time of man.

The beauty of the morning is not to be ignored,
             is there to uplift the spirit,
             is displayed to magnify the soul
                  as eyes are filled with wonder,
                  as eyes are seen to pause,
                  as eyes come to marvel at the surrounds of creation.

The beauty of the morning is visited upon both time and space,
             upon both the present and The Earth,
             upon both the just and the unjust.

The beauty of the morning is an adjunct of creation,
             is within the testimony of God to man,
             is at the forefront of the livelihood of man,
             is dynamic in design,
             is varied and delightful,
             is memorable and moving,
             is enhancing and exquisite.

The beauty of the morning overwrites the pains of yesterday,
             overwrites the pain of mourning,
             overwrites the trials found within mortality,
             overwrites the ugliness of sin,
             overwrites the scenes of misbehaviour,

overwrites with the seal of long-term approval emanating from
The God of placement who so loves the world.

The beauty of the morning is as grace disclosed,
is as grace encountered,
is as grace on offer.

The beauty of the morning knows the thunderstorms of life,
knows the erasing of the slates;
knows the turbulence found within the soul,
knows the calm found within The Spirit's wind;
knows the temptations of the spirit,
knows the forgiveness of God.

The beauty of the morning should be ascribed to God:
as it is destined for the awe of man.

The beauty of the morning is reflected in the face of man back to his God of Love."

My Content Study Aid

_____
_____
_____
_____
_____
_____
_____
_____
_____
_____
_____
_____
_____
_____
_____
_____
_____
_____

- ANTHONY A EDDY (SCRIBE)

The Bounty of The Earth

"The bounty of The Earth is at the beck and call of man.

The bounty of The Earth is subject to the fittest,
               is subject to the strongest,
               is subject to the richest,
               is subject to the greediest,
               is subject to the bravest,
               is subject to the most immoral.

The bounty of The Earth accrues to the mighty and the powerful,
                  the audacious and the keen,
                  the usurpers and the pillagers,
                  the plunderers and the pirates,
                  the benefactors and the wise,
                  the ignoble and the inquisitors.

The bounty of The Earth is scarcely served to the victims and the vanquished,
                     the impoverished and the impotent,
                     the hapless and the hopeless,
                     the senseless and the separated,
                     the wastrels and the wishful.

The bounty of The Earth verifies the provisioning for man,
               verifies the foresight of design,
               verifies the stores placed within the storehouse long before the
                                     need arose.

The bounty of The Earth leaves no need unmet,
               leaves the stores in place,
               leaves the stores held ready,
               leaves the stores with access,
               leaves the stores for functions as intended,
               leaves the stores as an inheritance for man.

The bounty of The Earth shares in the food of man;
               shares in his ability to explore;
               shares in his ability to freeze,
                   his ability to heat,
                   his ability to shine with his use of hands;
               shares in his preparation of his goods for trade.

The bounty of The Earth has extractions worth uplifting;
               has extractions to blend and measure;
               has extractions for the artefacts;
               has extractions destined for the stars,

the moons,
the planets known to man.

The bounty of The Earth serves the knowledge of man with equanimity;
serves up the solutions made known from the wisdom of God:
when and as combined with purpose of intent,
with design through insight,
with accidental exposures due to circumstance,
as labelled and thereby so claimed by man.

The bounty of The Earth can meet the needs of man solely by an act of the will of God
when the ears of man are filled with the noises of the world.

The bounty of The Earth is sufficient for the day of man:
for the aspirations of man,
for the growth of man.

The bounty of The Earth suffices man until the end-time attains completion:
when all is re-assessed."

My Content Study Aid

_____

_____

_____

_____

_____

_____

_____

_____

_____

_____

_____

_____

_____

_____

_____

_____

_____

_____

_____

The End-time Vacancies of My Spirit

"The end-time vacancies of My Spirit result
> in neglected opportunities lost from the preparation of man,
> in neglected opportunities of promise,
> in neglected opportunities of relationship,
> in neglected opportunities for selection of a destiny,
> in neglected opportunities of inheritance,
> in neglected opportunities arising through procrastination.

The end-time vacancies of My Spirit are found throughout The Earth;
> are found in all races,
> are found in all cultures,
> are found in all creeds:
> are found through non-belief,
> are found through partial belief,
> are found through misbelief.

The end-time vacancies of My Spirit are filled one at a time,
> are filled upon repentance,
> are filled upon commitment,
> are filled upon a testimony,
> are filled according to My word.

The end-time vacancies of My Spirit always has one more to fill the call
> from a wandering spirit,
> from a cry for help,
> from a rescue from the servitude of sin:
> to install redemption back into the framework built for man.

The end-time vacancies of My Spirit should receive an invitation to create a temple for a
> spirit and a soul—
> so My Spirit can dwell therein with man,
> so a relationship can be brought into existence,
> so an entry which qualifies can be entered in The Book of Life.

The end-time vacancies of My Spirit are fettered by the dominator of The Earth,
> by his myriads of dissemblers:
> by acceptance by man of the status quo of a soul domineering his spirit,
> of a body serving as an empty house:
> of The God of Love waiting in the wings
> for His call to centre stage.

The end-time vacancies of My Spirit should diminish before the end of time;
> cannot diminish after the end of time.

The end-time vacancies of My Spirit when filled repel the activities of demons,

the grand design of Satan,
the destiny of default.

The end-time vacancies of My Spirit speak of man's preparation,
of grace laid upon the table for communion as an offering to man,
of revelation from the throne room of God,
of revelation so none may perish,
of revelation to prevent the capture of man's soul and the death of his spirit,
of revelation to bring man understanding of his power to choose his destination.

The end-time vacancies of My Spirit greet with great joy each filled address of man as
each becomes a temple;
with an entry in The Book of Life:
made to ensure companionship with The Living God."

My Content Study Aid

_____
_____
_____
_____
_____
_____
_____
_____
_____
_____
_____
_____
_____
_____
_____
_____
_____
_____
_____
_____
_____
_____

- ANTHONY A EDDY (SCRIBE)

The End-time Wisdom on Time

"When in the absence of the pendulum of time,
  cause and effect are no longer linked,
    can be viewed in either order,
    can be viewed solely dependent on the will of the playwright of the scenes.

For as the effect is desired to be,
    so the cause can be ascribed into the reality of existence.
For as the cause is desired to be,
    so the effect can be ascribed into the reality of existence.*

Hence the first may be last and the last may be first when order is important.

The I AM of creation is the first and the last,
          the alpha and the omega,
          the beginning and the end:
                as He dwells outside the time of man.

When Heaven orchestrates the edifice of God so matters may happen simultaneously,
      yet man requires a sequence of relationships described within his time frame
                for the comprehension of his life upon The Earth.

Similarly is it necessary for his understanding of the structure of eternity:
            in terms familiar to the reality of his experience within mortality.

The clash of the cultures found on Earth with the cultures found in the heavens is severe
                    and complex when attempting to reconcile,
                    by way of explanation,
    the life style known to each in the concepts available in the languages of The Earth.

So the actions attributed to the seven seals,
  so the actions attributed to the seven bowls,
  so the actions attributed to the seven angels may not occur within the heavens in the
                sequencing of time as known to man;
  yet are so described within My word to enable the understanding of mortal man while
                          on The Earth."

Scribal Note: *These four lines of text are correct as they are.*

My Content Study Aid

_____

_____

_____

The End-time Visions of My People

"The visions of My people are not without a purpose,
                        are to be tested by My Spirit,
                        are to be authored by the being of God.

The valid visions of My people are to encourage,
                        are to edify,
                        are to testify.

The valid visions of My people are to bring change into a life,
                        are to enlist a spirit,
                        are to uplift a soul.

The valid visions of My people are not imparted to fall upon the dust,
                        are not given to be put into an archive,
                        are not imprinted to be just ignored.

The valid visions of My people are not a regular occurrence,
                        are not common to all identities,
                        are not seen unless selected for a message.

The valid visions of My people deserve their understanding,
                        deserve a written record,
                        deserve a path of progress,
                        deserve the implant of the intent,
                        deserve reference to a peer,
                        deserve a prayer in answer.

The valid visions of My people speak the spiritual into the physical,
                        speak from the oracle of God,
                        speak into the reception room of man.

The end-time visions of My people are to be discerned against a changing background,
                        are to be acknowledged according to My word,
                        are to be accepted within the field of grace.

The end-time visions of My people bring the aura of God to man,
                        bring an end-time message with clarity and distinction,
                        bring the attention of man to focus on the will of God.

The end-time visions of My people are reserved for this season of the clouds,
                        are reserved to instil the message inherent in the latter rains,
                        are reserved for the end-time preparation of man.

The end-time visions of My people confirm the validity of My bride,
                        the validity of My return,
                        the validity of kingdom rule,

- ANTHONY A EDDY (SCRIBE)

55

the validity of angels so prepared,
the validity of the approval of The Father,
the validity of the readiness of The Son,
the validity of My Spirit's preparation for the
vacant souls of man."

My Content Study Aid

_____

_____

_____

_____

_____

_____

_____

_____

_____

_____

_____

_____

_____

_____

_____

_____

_____

_____

_____

_____

_____

_____

_____

The Power of My People

"The power of My people is to be increased,
                is to be prepared in readiness,
                is for the rule and reign with Christ.

The power of My people is not a trite expression,
                is real and to the fore,
                is certain and determined,
                is convincing and sustained.

The power of My people is righteous and administrative,
                is ordered and constrained,
                is forbearing and discerning,
                is innovative and judicious.

The power of My people is circumspect and lawful,
                is indicative and confirmative,
                is helpful and assisting,
                is eager and auspicious.

The power of My people settles and distributes,
                summons and decides,
                queries and ascertains,
                listens and discloses.

The power of My people emanates from God,
                supports the edifice of God,
                upholds the glory of a kingdom known to God.

The power of My people has no intent of evil,
                has no agenda unknown to God,
                has no attachment to the residues of sin.

The power of My people is blessed and approved by God,
                is inherited from the throne room of God,
                is developed and enveloped by the love of God for man.

The power of My people is collective and assured,
                is sensitive and calming,
                is authoritative and disarming,
                is far reaching and impressive.

The power of My people surges and relaxes,
                concentrates and wanes,
                builds and climaxes,
                fragments and unites.

- ANTHONY A EDDY (SCRIBE)

The power of My people encompasses and assembles,
> fixes and breaks,
> claims and disowns,
> encircles and directs.

The power of My people visits and dismisses,
> comforts and supports,
> reinforces and repairs,
> inhabits and vacates.

The power of My people enters and retreats according to the scene,
>> according to the need,
>> according to the will of God.

The power of My people is in the fulfilment of the centuries,
> is in the promises of God,
> is in the crafting of the destiny of light.

The power of My people knows the handshake of creation,
> knows the presence of their God,
> knows the inheritance of The Son conveyed to the bridal saints
>> which be."

My Content Study Aid

_____

_____

_____

_____

_____

_____

_____

_____

_____

_____

_____

_____

_____

The End-time Curtain of The Veil

"The curtain of the veil has been in place for centuries,
    has been in place to protect the mysteries of God,
    has been in place to enshroud until release.

The curtain of the veil is as eyelids firmly closed upon the eyes,
    as curtains drawn across the windows of the soul,
    as darkness of intent which does not transmit the light.

The curtain of the veil can be opened partially in stages as if upon a stage,
    can give access as if through blinkers on a horse,
    can give access as if through a skylight in a roof,
    can give access as if from the bottom of a well,
    can give access as if with a telescope with a narrow field of view,
    can give access as if in the middle of the night,
    can give access as if lit by the risen sun.

The curtain of the veil controls the view of man;
    controls viewing access to another realm:
    controls the smoke as in a smoke screen,
    controls the fog as in a foggy day,
    controls the mist as in a misty morning which dissipates upon the
        arrival of the sun.

The curtain of the veil is readied for an act of disclosure,
    has the approval of The Father,
    has the acknowledgment of The Son,
    has the affirmation of the preparation of The Spirit to so move
        the veil.

The curtain of the veil is so designed to control the interplay of light and sound onto the
        sensors of man.

The curtain of the veil is as an aurora for the mind of man which selectively displays at
        the will of God.

The curtain of the veil is functional and operational,
    was programmed for exclusion,
    is soon to be modified for the end-time revelations,
        for the end-time comings,
        for the end-time advent of The Lord."

- ANTHONY A EDDY (SCRIBE)

59

The End-time Power of God

"The end-time power of God is to be no longer limited by self-imposition,
is to be no longer limited in His tending of man,
is to be no longer limited in His approach to evil,
is to be no longer limited by the expression of grace,
is to be no longer limited upon The Earth,
is to be no longer limited as His kingdom comes,
is to be no longer limited by The Father and The Son.

The end-time power of God is to be displayed for all to see,
is to be displayed for all to hear,
is to be displayed for all to know.

The end-time power of God unleashes the wrath of God
on man standing on intransigence,
on man recoiling from the offered grace,
on man blinded to his surrounding proof of presence,
on man circumscribed by intellect,
on man who dwells not in the land of faith,
on man committed to his idols before the face of God.

The end-time power of God discards such to their graves;
discards such to the destiny of default;
discards such to the second death:
discards such so imperilled when unvisited by repentance,
discards such so imperilled outside the mantle of The
Covenant anew.

The end-time power of God seizes and destroys,
prepares and protects,
justifies and sanctifies.

The end-time power of God redeems and restores,
calls and welcomes,
drafts and separates.

The end-time power of God acknowledges and respects,
rewards and restricts,
instates and confines.

The end-time power of God prepares the throne rooms of God for the presence of The
Faithful as in The Book of Life."

The End-time Mortality of Man

"The end-time mortality of man sees history at a turning point,
                sees history impacted again by God,
                sees history continued into immortality.

The end-time mortality of man opens the door into eternity:
                the door into the presence of God;
                the door of the entryway to Hell.

The end-time mortality of man seizes The Saints of God together with The Lost of spirit,
                soul,
                and body.

The end-time mortality of man is in the time of preparation:
    of learning not to succumb to the immediate fear of man,
    of receiving knowledge of the new parameters of life,
    of seeking the new prospects of being as companions to
            the stars,
    of turning from the past and future concepts into the
            timelessness of the present,
    of coping with the distant visitations on offer,
of equipping with the discovered patterns of existence furnishing the environment
    of the presence of man now at home within the family of God.

The end-time mortality of man is a time for the discovery of the clues of God:
    clues to expand the understanding of The
        Faithful of eternity and of The Lost in time,
    clues as to the coming experiences of man,
    clues shed from the mysteries of God,
    clues to the changed conditions of man,
    clues to might and majesty revealed,
    clues as to what the expectations of man may
        so aspire to as he journeys on.

The end-time mortality of man sheds light into his being in the present:
    sheds light or darkness upon his destiny as selected,
    sheds answers to the sheep,
    sheds redeeming knowledge to the goats,
    sheds faith unto the faithless,
    sheds commitment to the ignorant of purpose.

The end-time mortality of man sheds grace so it everywhere abounds,
    sheds grace in its time of being to the fore,
    sheds grace so the penitent may firmly grasp the promise
        prior to the closure of the age.

- ANTHONY A EDDY (SCRIBE)

The end-time mortality of man approaches as a threshold,
                    approaches as a new beginning,
                    approaches with the engulfing of a time warp,
                    approaches with the two Kingdom keys—
                              entrusted by The Father unto His Son—
                                  which either fit the door to Heaven
                                    or the door to Hell,
                    approaches with the choice determined from within the
                              freewill agency of man,
                    approaches when the freewill of man is either to be
                              honoured or to be respected.

The end-time mortality of man encircles the end-time harvest,
                    gathers the latent saints-in-waiting,
                    welcomes those with the committing of the soul unto the
                              light of Christ."

My Content Study Aid

_____

_____

_____

_____

_____

_____

_____

_____

_____

_____

_____

_____

_____

_____

_____

_____

_____

_____

The End-time Casting of The Net

"The end-time casting of the net has a degree of urgency,
>> has a degree of completion of a calling,
>> has a degree of rescuing the extremities of man.

The end-time casting of the net lets the slippery fall through,
>> lets the vain gaze at the stars,
>> lets the predators thrash on the surface,
>> lets the slothful feed at the bottom,
>> lets the travellers speed on their way.

The end-time casting of the net gathers in those waiting in their place,
>> those hoping for a change in life,
>> those expecting a better birthright.

The end-time casting of the net gathers in the inquisitive and the mindful,
>> the festive and the gay,
>> the happy and the tearful,
>> the victim and the villain,
>> the mud-lark and the preener,
>> the follower and the leader.

The end-time casting of the net gathers in the doubtful and the sceptic,
>> the sinner and the saint,
>> the agnostic and the religious,
>> the idolater and the ignorant,
>> the bashful and the proud,
>> the wanderer and the wounded.

The end-time casting of the net serves each with the waters of life,
>> an introduction to the King of kings,
>> the option of commitment,
>> the promise of a life beyond the present
>> bounds of man.

The end-time casting of the net reveals to the inhabitants the reality of God:
>> the availability of fresh food for the soul,
>> of fresh thoughts for the spirit,
>> of fresh caring for the body.

The end-time casting of the net is an act of love,
>> does not seek the reward of man,
>> would uplift all to a higher plane.

The end-time casting of the net serves and satisfies the hunger of the soul,
>> the thirsting of the spirit,
>> the supervision of the shell indwelt.

- ANTHONY A EDDY (SCRIBE)

The end-time casting of the net answers and elicits,

prevents and opens up,
displays and transforms,
shapes and moulds,
builds and anchors,
guides and teaches.

The end-time casting of the net prepares the soul for fitting with a new set of clothes,

prepares the soul of man for the guidance of the spirit
of man,
prepares the spirit of man for the companionship of The
Spirit of God,
prepares the body of man for transitioning from the grave.

The end-time casting of the net leads in a quest for attainment of knowledge of the truth,

for attainment of a relationship with God,
for attainment of the reality of the life
beyond the grave.

The end-time casting of the net confirms the practicality of the love of God,

of the sacrifice of the living God,
of the redemptive power of the eternal God.

The end-time casting of the net calls for a response which leads to adoption into the
ongoing family of God."

My Content Study Aid

_____

_____

_____

_____

_____

_____

_____

_____

_____

_____

_____

_____

The End-time Passion of The Lord

"The end-time passion of The Lord is soon to soak The Earth,
is soon to bring new life,
is soon to bring fertility unto the barren and the
waste lands.

The end-time passion of The Lord is the song of victory,
is the fulfilment of grace,
is the shout of jubilation,
is the cry of angels,
is the scent of The Spirit,
is the promise of The Father:
all vested on the children of God.

The end-time passion of The Lord surrounds His return,
amplifies His status,
magnifies His presence,
builds upon His glory,
raises the bride unto the clouds of conquest,
sequesters Satan out of reach.

The end-time passion of The Lord changes the perspective of saints,
validates the faith of saints,
enhances the vision of saints,
sounds the call to man,
progresses on His journeying with man.

The end-time passion of The Lord realizes His inheritance from The Father,
the integrity of The Spirit,
the coming-forth of The Son upon The Earth.

The end-time passion of The Lord establishes and ordains,
rejoices and broadcasts,
publishes and proclaims.

The end-time passion of The Lord sees the rider on the white horse upon the land,
sees the bow in use with arrows as offered
for selection,
sees the impaling of the targets with the message for
the hearts.

The end-time passion of The Lord sees communion on a scale beyond the envisaging
of man,
sees the heights from which the crowns descend,
sees the end-time beautification of the saints—
as each stands before the beautifier of The Earth in a bridal role.

- ANTHONY A EDDY (SCRIBE)

The end-time passion of The Lord redecorates The Earth to the highest standard,
refurbishes and repairs,
restores newness to the shopworn,
restores acceptance to rejection,
restores forgiveness to embitterment;
restores God upon His throne with man,
restores man into His garden with God:
restores companionship to both in righteousness
and peace.

The end-time passion of The Lord redeems The Earth from Satan into its intended glory."

My Content Study Aid

_____

_____

_____

_____

_____

_____

_____

_____

_____

_____

_____

_____

_____

_____

_____

_____

_____

_____

_____

_____

_____

_____

The End-time Settlement of Man

"The end-time settlement of man speaks of his disposition
> both on and throughout The Earth,
> both physical and mental,
> both secular and sacred.

The end-time settlement of man tests his reserves of strength,
> tests his preparedness,
> tests his mind-set occasioned by freewill.

The end-time settlement of man speaks of his commitment to his intellect,
> his commitment to the ways of others,
> his commitment to the ways of God.

The end-time settlement of man can reflect the insinuations of the wiles of Satan,
> can absorb the insinuations of the devil,
> can espouse the insinuations of the demons.

The end-time settlement of man may be under the auspices of man,
> may be under the auspices of Satan,
> may be under the auspices of God.

The end-time settlement of man should have an eye single to the glory of God:
> should be disposed to walk with God,
> should be disposed to dwell within the fear of God,
> should be disposed to commune with God.

The end-time settlement of man is at risk when settling for less than the counselling
> of God,
> for less than the wisdom of God,
> for less than the active presence
> of God:
> within a life within mortality.

The end-time settlement of man is fraught with danger of continued existence
> when bereft of knowledge of the end-time of man,
> when bereft of preparation so to recognize the end-time signs,
> when bereft of foresight due to cope with the great tribulation;
> befalling man in his heyday of success.

The end-time settlement of man should address the six-fold dispositions of man,
> should have wisdom to attest to each,
> should be aware of the peril of his position if freewill-
> running-amok pounds on the door of
> he who stands to flail at shadows,
> who is filled with self-pity on the day of his accounting,

- ANTHONY A EDDY (SCRIBE)

who assumes the consequences of the days of slothfulness,
who dies in a house of cards built on a foundation of
compacted sin.

The end-time settlement of man should seek the sacred and the divine,
the blesséd and the true,
the righteous and the mantled—
so that peace may dwell under the covering of an entry in The Book of Life:
that which testifies of commitment to The God of destinies,
to The Lord of Hosts,
to The I AM of the heavens
and of The Earth."

My Content Study Aid

_____
_____
_____
_____
_____
_____
_____
_____
_____
_____
_____
_____
_____
_____
_____
_____
_____
_____
_____

The Holiness of God (2)

"The holiness of God is protected with great sensitivity,
        does not suffer the casualness of contempt,
        will not prolong a relationship where reverence is absent,
        will not instruct with wisdom when fear is not present in the heart.

The holiness of God is declared within the silence,
        is made known to those who wait upon The Lord,
        is present as if a white tablecloth upon a table when in the setting of
                          The Spirit.

The holiness of God does not retreat,
        does not intrude;
        is there to be approached by the humbled righteous,
        is there to be approached by those who know their God,
        is there to be approached where a close relationship exists.

The holiness of God is sensitive to sin howsoever carried by man,
        is sensitive to whosoever advances to the altar,
        is sensitive to unclean hands engaging in a role requiring sanctity.

The holiness of God knows the sacrifice of self,
        rewards the sacrifice of self,
        understands the love required to see to completion the sacrifice
                          of self.

The holiness of God knows all the hidden secrets of man while in his imperfection,
        knows all of which to be ashamed,
        knows all which brings reward,
        knows all which brings disqualification to walk in the garden of
                          The Son.

The holiness of God sees through the fog banks of man,
             the smoke screens of man,
             the lies of man.

The holiness of God cannot be approached by man when man remains surrounded by the
                    tiers of his fog banks,
                    the envelopes of his smoke screens,
                    the forest of his unrepentant lies.

The holiness of God is not for the charlatan and the knave—
                until committed to be bathed in purity:
                    by the water of new life,
                    and The Spirit sent to counsel.

The holiness of God is not open to entreaty;

- ANTHONY A EDDY (SCRIBE)

knows all there is to know;

does not forget,

does not overlook either the 'fors' or the 'againsts' in a presentation
of an opened heart of faith;
of a cry of anguish,
of a shout in anger,
of a whisper of deceit,
of a mouth speaking with the complete integrity of My Spirit.

The holiness of God is such that man should approach in full preparedness,
in the readiness of his spirit,
in the readiness of his soul,
in the readiness of his body,
in the readiness of a relationship
established in honour,
in fear,
in humbleness sincere.

The holiness of God has access granted at the will of God,
cannot be bypassed in a hurry,
already knows the needs and urgencies of man.

The holiness of God stood,
stands,
continues;

was,
is,
continues;

impeached,
impeaches,
continues.

The holiness of God sets the standard of existence,
sets the standard for creation,
sets the standard due upon The Earth."

Scribal Note:
(2) Denotes this as a second item with the same name as an earlier one.
*Refer '*The Holiness of God *in His 3rd book* 'GOD Speaks as His Spirit Empowers*'*

My Content Study Aid

_____

_____

_____

The End-time Investiture of Man

"The end-time investiture of man is a ceremony of awards,
　　　　　　　is a ceremony of rewards,
　　　　　　　is a ceremony of honouring the freewill of man.

The end-time investiture of man is in the presence of The King of thorns,
　　　　　　　of The King stapled to the cross,
　　　　　　　of The King delivering grace,
　　　　　　　of The King bringing reconciliation,
　　　　　　　of The King sacrificing for the sins of man.

The end-time investiture of man derives from The Father's gift of a sacrificial son.

The end-time investiture of man results from righteousness within freewill,
　　　　　　　from justification within the fire of grace,
　　　　　　　from the counselling within My Spirit's presence,
　　　　　　　from the gifts of God served unto the prophets,
　　　　　　　from communion within the nurturing of the loving God.

The end-time investiture of man sees the glory of God shed upon His servants,
　　　　　　　sees the majesty of God wrought upon His servants,
　　　　　　　sees the authority of God shared upon His servants,
　　　　　　　sees the inheritance of God bestowed upon His servants,
　　　　　　　sees the love of God declared upon His servants.

The end-time investiture of man sees the fullness of reward,
　　　　　　　the fullness of knowledge,
　　　　　　　the fullness of adoption,
　　　　　　　the fullness of being,
　　　　　　　the fullness of the presence inherent in investiture:
　　　　　　　from the household of faith into the family of God.

The end-time investiture of man is a promise in fulfilment,
　　　　　　　is the open door to the place prepared,
　　　　　　　is the finishing line of the race,
　　　　　　　is the prize commensurate with the goal of graduation
　　　　　　　　　　from the journey of discipleship,
　　　　　　　is the 'welcome home' from all who guarded and
　　　　　　　　　　projected through the time in preparation.

The end-time investiture of man sees the proclamations of the banners waving in unison,
　　　　　　　　　　in victory,
　　　　　　　　　　in among the stars.

The end-time investiture of man acknowledges the faithfulness of God,
　　　　　　　the presence of the bride,
　　　　　　　the culmination of His church age as placed in the hands of man."

- ANTHONY A EDDY (SCRIBE)

The End-time Supremacy of God

"The end-time supremacy of God is assured and certain within the lives of His saints.

The end-time supremacy of God is doubted and confused by the dwellers in the
wilderness of man.

The end-time supremacy of God is known yet denied by the archives of evil.

The end-time supremacy of God looses and binds according to His will,
according to His word,
according to the layering of The Holy Spirit.

The end-time supremacy of God is resurgent on The Earth,
is reinstated in authority at the end-time signing-off of
Satan's season of dominion,
is reclaimed on The Earth after man's freewill
lies exposed to view,
lies exposed to centuries of rule,
lies exposed to his grand alliance,
lies exposed to the blood oaths
formed with the
house of horrors.

The end-time supremacy of God will address the idolatry of man;
will address the sinning of man on man:
will address the subjugation brought,
the enslaving of life,
the terror of compliance,
the muscles of the mighty,
the sowings of the selfish,
the gardens of the greedy,
the molesting of the minors,
the dawning of the day.

The end-time supremacy of God sees the honouring of righteousness,
the justice of integrity,
the instilling and installing of a kingdom's rule.

The end-time supremacy of God sees the vanquishing of lies,
the establishment of truth.

The end-time supremacy of God denotes great significance in the surroundings of the
ongoing lives of man,
of the ongoing being of the saints.

The end-time supremacy of God brings no fear to the fearing,
brings great fear to the fearful.

The end-time supremacy of God tallies and testifies,
> harnesses and hampers,
> uplifts and instructs.

The end-time supremacy of God bears witness to the loving,
> cares for those within the fold,
> salvages the wheat entwined with the tares,
> separates His sheep from the unbidden goats.

The end-time supremacy of God oversees His Kingdom in the full will of The Father,
> in the full light of The Son,
> in the fullness of The Spirit.

The end-time supremacy of God presents in might and majesty,
> in glory and magnificence,
> in trial and tribulation.

The end-time supremacy of God tends The Earth so it shall be fit for rule on The Son-rise
> of the day."

My Content Study Aid

_____
_____
_____
_____
_____
_____
_____
_____
_____
_____
_____
_____
_____
_____
_____
_____
_____
_____

- ANTHONY A EDDY (SCRIBE)

The Judgment of God

"The judgment of God brings fear unto the soul,
            brings fear unto the spirit,
            brings fear unto the countenance of man.

The judgment of God segregates and dissipates,
            sections and divides,
            impeaches and imprisons.

The judgment of God terminates and terrifies,
            silences and separates,
            gathers and gestates.

The judgment of God verifies and validates,
            casts and constricts,
            mandates and managers.

The judgment of God locates the ungodly of The Earth,
            destroys the sinning of the present,
            sequesters the slate-bearer of the record.

The judgment of God verifies the vanquished,
            punishes the pugnacious,
            indicts the invidious.

The judgment of God lists the lascivious,
            reaps the rapacious,
            severs the salacious.

The judgment of God superimposes death upon a life,
            superimposes suffering on a station,
            superimposes torment on the tangible.

The judgment of God maximizes the savagery of the silent soul,
            maximizes the solitude of the silent spirit,
            maximizes the begging of the battered body.

The judgment of God minimizes the language of the liars,
            minimizes the might of the minority,
            minimizes the frailty of the fallacious.

The judgment of God circulates amidst the causes,
            navigates amidst the nervous,
            tabulates amidst the testimonies.

The judgment of God releases man among the rats,
            releases man among the residues,
            releases man among the retributions.

The judgment of God closes on the conflicts,
>   closes on the captives,
>   closes on the conspicuous,
>   closes on the cautious,
>   closes on the capitulated,
>   closes on the conquered,
>   closes on the concealed,
>   closes on the contrite of confession.

The judgment of God closes on the estate of wisdom,
>   closes on the estate of rewards,
>   closes on the estate of inheritance:
>   closes on the estates protected by the covenantal promises of God."

My Content Study Aid

_____

_____

_____

_____

_____

_____

_____

_____

_____

_____

_____

_____

_____

_____

_____

_____

_____

_____

_____

_____

_____

_____

The End-time Wrath of God

"The end-time wrath of God changes the makeup of The Earth,
    moves the mountains of accountability,
    alters the characters of man.

The end-time wrath of God reseeds The Earth with vigour,
    removes the sources of enmity to God,
    challenges the end-time beliefs of the saints of God.

The end-time wrath of God empties the bowls and fulfils the prophecies,
    inundates the lowlands and bakes the hinterlands,
    measures the faith and quantifies the discipleship.

The end-time wrath of God surveys the worriers and despatches the warriors,
    values the knowledgable and preserves the wise of God,
    proclaims the freewill destined for respect and testifies of the
        freewill destined for full honour.

The end-time wrath of God vindicates the mistreated and uplifts the humble,
    falls on the warring of The Earth and terrifies the captains of
        industry misusing trust,
    demolishes the satanic emblems and safeguards the
        sanctuaries of God.

The end-time wrath of God wraps up the objectors and disposes of the charlatans,
    seeks the mouths of blasphemy and finds the hands
        of idolatry,
    curtails the warned and diminishes the disobedient.

The end-time wrath of God services the righteous and gratifies the just,
    leads the companionable and encourages the repentant,
    fills the vacant and replenishes the dispirited.

The end-time wrath of God purifies The Earth ready for the bride and magnifies The
    Kingdom ready for The King."

My Content Study Aid

_____

_____

_____

_____

_____

The End-time Blessing of My Lands

"I,
   The Lord,
      speak to My servants,
         as they approach My Lands.

I,
   The Lord,
      speak to My servants,
         as they are prepared to meet My Lands head on—
               with all My Lands have in store—
               with all My Lands have accumulated:
                     by way of dross,
                     by way of precious jewels,
                     by way of the temples of My Spirit.

I,
   The Lord,
      ask of My servants this day:
         that they will ignite The Spirit's flame in the lives of My saints,
         that they will persevere amongst the strongholds of the foe of man,
         that they will break the curses as they encounter lives in darkness—
            the darkness over My Lands which suffer the bondage,
               the captivity of the souls with the spirits of man—
                  attacked and diminished from their being at creation.

My servants free,
My servants liberate,
My servants introduce:
   to testify of their presence through their end-time callings,
               in their lands of tasking,
               by My Spirit's leading.

My servants know the closets in need of cleaning with the broom of My Spirit—
         that which impales the demons on the bristles bringing them to no effect and
                 prepared for disposal of their influence on their
                 being in the precincts of the Temples of The Lord.

My servants bind and loose with great effect in each land of promise—
               so houses may be cleansed,
               so the broken are redeemed,
               so the sick are restored to health,
               so those of little faith see,
                     hear,
                     believe,

- ANTHONY A EDDY (SCRIBE)

77

as they witness My Spirit in action in their lives.

My servants approach boldly to rebut,
> approach with single-mindedness of intent,
> approach bearing the decrees of God:
>> at which the demons will pack their bags to leave for other climes.

My servants are prepared and armed for the repelling of the darkness—
> that which they are not called to skirt—
> in their land of blessing:
> in their land of blessing where their footprints are to be both seen
>> and felt."

My Content Study Aid

_____

_____

_____

_____

_____

_____

_____

_____

_____

_____

_____

_____

_____

_____

_____

_____

_____

_____

_____

The End-time Need of My People

"My people need to know the fullness of My Spirit—
>> need to be introduced to that with which they are unfamiliar—
>> need to have upon their lips the vocabularies of God.

My people need an erstwhile communication with their God established and in place.

My people need the sign of My Spirit present in their lives,
>>> present in their children,
>>> present in the being of each day presented to them.

My people need the first-hand experience of knowing I am with them,
>>> of knowing how to reach Me,
>>> of knowing how to speak with certainty to their
>>>> listening God.

My people need the blessings of the tongues of Heaven which are not for man to
>>> withhold from man.

My people shall receive,
> each in their own appointed time,
>> the cascading of My waterfalls of tongues upon the deserts and the plains where
>>> they remain unknown—
>>> as the vessels know not for which they search.

My people are in need of My Spirit's Counsel uninterpreted by man.

For these are the days God speaks directly with His people."

My Content Study Aid

_____
_____
_____
_____
_____
_____
_____
_____
_____
_____

- ANTHONY A EDDY (SCRIBE)

The End-time Threshold of God

"Well-wishers on birthdays mark the passage of the years,
                 mark an anniversary of a birth,
                 mark in recognition the character so formed.

Of all man may achieve upon a birthday,
         character is at the forefront when presented at the threshold of God.

Character sees the stumble of weakness,
         sees the certainty of righteousness in the placing of the footsteps in the
                                         sun light,
         sees the protection from the nighthawk—
                 where he does not fly at night.

The threshold of God,
  the welcome mat of God,
  the door where the seekers knock,
  the access to the doors with the kingdom locks—
         with the kingdom keys—
         with the binding and the loosing as they are turned to the left or
                                     to the right.

This is the starting point of man's relationship with God,
         of God's relationship with man.

This is where man meets Grace.

This is where God encounters freewill declared.

Such as these are not dependent on the anniversaries of man,
         are not dependent on the wisdom of man,
         are not dependent on the striving of man:
         are dependent on nothing but a contrite heart."

My Content Study Aid

_____
_____
_____
_____
_____
_____

The End-time Days of Pentecost

"The days of pentecost are about to revisit The Earth of man,
    are about to circumnavigate The Earth of man,
    are about to re-enlist the saints of God on The Earth of man.

The days of pentecost are about to seize the days of Satan from before his throne,
    are about to re-awaken the souls of God,
    are about to bring the dry bones up from the valleys.

The days of pentecost are about to call the penitent before the throne of God.

The days of pentecost are about to see the penitent,
    the dry bones,
    the souls of God,
    aflame with My Spirit's fire,
    aflame with My Spirit's holiness,
    aflame with the fear of God,
    emboldened with the voice of God,
    emboldened with the will of God,
    emboldened with the searchlight of My Spirit.

For the searchlight of My Spirit is as the x-ray machine of God for man,
    is as the plumber of the depths of man,
    is as the examiner of the body,
    soul,
    and spirit,
    of the character,
    heart,
    and mind—
    for righteousness—
    for a relationship with God—
    for an accord with God.

For the accord with God denotes a new covenant in place whereby the being of man,
    in all completeness,
    will be subject to full honour,
    will encounter all the promises,
    will be qualified for his inheritance from God.

For these days of pentecost are of relevance to the advent of The Lord.

For these days of the return of pentecost in its fullness are the days of My Spirit's witness
    of the end-time to the saints of God.

For these days are not the days for the unprepared,
    for those of little faith,

- ANTHONY A EDDY (SCRIBE)

81

> for those with a foot planted in both camps,
> for those who doubt,
> for those in denial.

For these are the days when the saints of God will stand in service.

For these are the days when the goats will flee,
> when the lambs will have no milk,
> when the shepherds will be mindful of His sheep—
> > who each knows his walk of faith,
> > > of righteousness,
> > > of grace.

For as each has sought so each will receive.

For as each has attained so each will be rewarded.

For as each knows the shepherd so each will be claimed."

My Content Study Aid

_____

_____

_____

_____

_____

_____

_____

_____

_____

_____

_____

_____

_____

_____

_____

_____

_____

_____

The End-time Teardrops of My Children

"The teardrops of My children are not lightly shed,
                are not lightly left to roll down upon a face,
                are not lightly left in place.

The teardrops of My children are not dependent upon age,
                are not dependent upon gender,
                are not dependent upon the wealth of man.

The teardrops of My children arise from their sense of being,
                deep within the soul,
                when emotions are to the fore.

The teardrops of My children arise from a state of desertion,
                from a state of loneliness,
                from a state of forlornness,
                from a state of separation,
                from a state of lost hope,
                from a state of need unsatisfied.

The teardrops of My children arise from a scene of battering,
                arise from a scene of beating,
                arise from a scene of subjugation,
                arise from a scene of injustice,
                arise from a scene of rejection,
                arise from a scene of arousal.

The teardrops of My children speak of a need known within My kingdom,
                a need for protection,
                a need for discernment,
                a need to mend a broken fence,
                a need to take corrective action,
                a need to stop the turning of a blinded eye.

The teardrops of My children are the evidence of things astray,
                are the evidence of stress incurred,
                are the evidence of failure to comply,
                are the evidence of a lack of light,
                are the evidence of revolving round a mountain,
                are the evidence of broken communications.

The teardrops of My children are never forsaken,
        write their records in The Lamb's Book of Life,
                will each be addressed in the day of accountability,
                will each bear witness in The Land of mercy,
                will each seek justice for what has been denied,

- ANTHONY A EDDY (SCRIBE)

83

will each bring light into the darkness of a soul.

The teardrops of The Saints are not matters of little import,
>   are tended with close attention:
>   have angels attending to comfort the distressed,
>   are each recorded on a slate containing terms for an erasure.

The teardrops of The Saints are attended to with alacrity,
>   are attended to with precision,
>   are attended to in order not to result in damage to the spirit,
>   damage to the body,
>   damage to the soul.

The teardrops of The Saints,
>   of My children,
>   of the sons and daughters of God,
>   are not permitted to challenge their walk with God,
>   their destiny with God,
>   their relationship with God,
>   through the attacks of Satan."

My Content Study Aid

_____

_____

_____

_____

_____

_____

_____

_____

_____

_____

_____

_____

_____

_____

My End-time Ministry of My Servants

"The waywardness of man is not counted against My servants.

The slips of the tongue of man,
>> the stumbles of his feet,
>>> the misplacement of his hands are not counted against My servants in this age
>>>> of grace.

My children still are blessed by the guidance uttered by the mouths of My servants in the
>> presence of their hearts' intent.

The intent of each heart in prayer to free a captive is the act of faith,
>> is the act of obedience,
>>> is the act of honour which stands before the throne awaiting the support
>>>> of God.

The guidance,
> uttered by the mouths of My servants,
>> falls on the ears of the supplicants for the building of their faith,
>>> for the speaking to their souls,
>>> for the uplifting of their spirits.

My servants minister in the will of God,
> within the guidance,
>> the knowledge,
>> the wisdom of the day:
>>> which impacts on the soul,
>>>> the spirit,
>>> and the body of the supplicant—
>>> who seeks the attention of God for an act of grace."

My Content Study Aid

_____

_____

_____

_____

_____

_____

_____

_____

The End-time Ecology of Man

"The skills of man are insufficient to avert the wrath of God.

The skills of man are but as if a child playing at the beach.

The skills of man impress no one on The Earth but man.

The skills of man are harnessed,
>>are manipulated,
>>>are skewed by Satan for the destruction of man in the twilight of
>>>>>>>>his career.

The career of man is filled with his careering,
>>>that which is not to his credit,
>>>that which leads him nowhere but downwards,
>>>that which assembles the cheerers who become the jeerers.

The jeerers of The Earth have membership in the satanic forces,
>>>have membership in the body of man,
>>>have membership of the club known as The Souls of Satan,
>>>have membership through the consensus of ill-will to man
>>>>>>through the key of self-promotion,
>>>have membership which gratifies the lusts of man,
>>>have membership which denies them access to the God
>>>>>>>>of righteousness.

The souls of Satan have had their time within the sunlight,
>>>have had their times of prosperity which is little recompense,
>>>have had their times within earshot of the warning bells of God,
>>>have had their backs turned—
>>>>>to face the shadows,
>>>have had their mouths turned into caves of blasphemy,
>>>have had their whitened souls of childhood with the spirits which
>>>>>>>>were free—
>>>>changed into their latter blackened souls with each spirit
>>>>>>>>fully captured.

So as man is lost to God,
>>as man falls beyond redemptive reach,
>>as man succumbs to Satan,
>>>>so his destiny becomes assured as the bells toll,
>>>>>>>>by way of confirmation—
>>>>>the timing of man for entry to the grave.

The souls of man have chosen their outlets of freewill,
>>>>their outlets of great shame,
>>>>their outlets beyond the reach of trumpets,

their outlets with the reward of promise,
their outlets which all lead to an alley which is blind,
which has no exit,
which has no light,
which has the entrance closed
for those who would retreat.

The souls of man leave the field of play with the field in tatters,
with the field deserted,
with the field no longer nourished,
with the field no longer able to nourish the days
of man.

The souls of man pillage without foresight,
pillage without wisdom,
pillage for the sake of feeding on corruption,
of feeding on the now,
of feeding leaving nothing as an inheritance
for the generations forced to move,
for the generations whose livelihood is lost,
for the generations without a sequence of provision.

The souls of man plunder for the purse strings,
relinquish when tribute can no longer be extracted,
dismiss without a care for what is left behind.

The souls of man motivate the churlish,
enforce their secularity,
diminish responsibility,
deny accountability,
leave little of any worth,
vacate the sites ransacked by the greedy.

The souls of man in such a plight are not known by God,
are not the harbingers of freedom,
are not on the upward gradients of light,
are not gifted with the tools of God,
are not numbered among His servants,
are not enabled to accomplish wonders.

The sequence of accomplishment arises from a foundation instilled from God,
from a foundation which calls on revelation,
which is built on the rock of revelation,
which knows not the sinking sands of failure;
from a foundation laid by My Spirit,
from a foundation of My word,
from a foundation known to God containing
precious stones.

- ANTHONY A EDDY (SCRIBE)

The sequence of accomplishment results in gratitude and benefit,
    results in multitudes at rest,
    results in environments enhanced,
    results in each daybreak bringing hope,
    results in each dusk fulfilling happiness.

The sequence of accomplishment should be tested for the fruit;
    for it is in the fruit of the effort of man—
        of the life of man,
    that the origin is determined,
    that the origin is declared to all who would test:
        to all who would know whether destined
            for the gold preserving great glory,
        or for the straw found blowing in the wind.

The God of nations restores and redeems,
    selects and builds,
    teaches and trains,
    knows and uplifts.

The God of nations verifies and punishes,
    angers and calls to account,
    seeks truth and righteousness in man.

The God of nations monitors the mistakes of man,
    reclothes The Earth,
    restocks the seas,
    refurbishes the dwelling place of man."

My Content Study Aid

_____

_____

_____

_____

_____

_____

_____

_____

_____

_____

The End-time Relay Centres of My Temples

"My people are presently not adept at hearing the voice of God,
at being on the wavelength of transmission,
at clearing the static which distorts reception,
at listening until it is the time to speak,
at conveying the intent of God with a
message unadulterated.

My people should attempt to communicate on the wavelengths used by God,
the wavelengths of the tongues of My Spirit,
the wavelengths of thought outside the bounds of time,
the wavelengths built for the flash drives of the memory
with no moving parts,
the wavelengths faster than the light slowed by its
presence in the realm of physics.

My people are in the end-time of their preparation,
are encouraged to acquire the gifts of the fullness of The Spirit,
the promise of The Father,
the transmission mode of the angels:
the firewire of the heavens.

My people are encouraged to increase their abilities among the vocabularies of
the heavens,
to not dawdle in the solitude still with the tongue of initiation,
to explore the field of tongues where every blade protruding—
feeds both the spirit and the soul,
surprises the body on hearing the power within the tongue,
declares the glory of achievement as progression is experienced,
comprises the summation of achievement as the temple starts transmission,
as the temple starts receiving,
as the temple starts interpreting,
as the temple starts translating
thoughts into the languages
of the stars of God.

The temple which receives and transmits readily,
freely with instant access,
across the frequencies of the languages of tongues,
as showered by The Spirit,
is then prepared for venturing into the life realm of the mode which carries the
voice of God in holiness and fear.

My Spirit hones and sharpens the tongues of My people,
tests and trains the tongues of My people,

- ANTHONY A EDDY (SCRIBE)

89

strengthens and exercises the tongues of My people,
bestows fluency with practise on the tongues of My people,
corrects the vocal cords for accents in the tongues of My people,
modifies by adjustment for pronunciation of the tongues of My people.

My Spirit qualifies the speakers for both clarity and pitch,
qualifies the speakers for conciseness and precision,
qualifies the speakers for accuracy and content,
qualifies the speakers by tuning in the station of The Voice.

My Spirit is the technician in the sound booth,
the technician in the vision centre,
the technician of the heavens which guides,
directs,
the temple communications to and from the throne room of God."

My Content Study Aid

_____
_____
_____
_____
_____
_____
_____
_____
_____
_____
_____
_____
_____
_____
_____
_____
_____
_____
_____

The End-time Catalysts of Destiny

"The movement of man as he approaches God,
                as he distances himself from God,
                are the catalysts of destiny which impact on the soul,
                                which greet the spirit,
                                which put postures on the body.

Something so simple as a whisper in an ear,
                as a drumbeat on a street,
                as a life event of the heart:
                        can lead to a life of luxury—
                                a life of luxury with God,
                                or a life of luxury alone.

Something so simple as a barb embedded in the flesh,
                as a stagger in the night,
                as a rejection of a dream:
                        can trigger a life of penury—
                                a life of penury with God,
                                or a life of penury in despair.

Something so simple as a kiss upon a cheek,
                as an emblem around a neck,
                as a stirring of a heart:
                        can establish a life of fulfilment—
                                a life of fulfilment with God,
                                or a life of fulfilment serving man.

The end-time catalysts of destiny are subject to the incurring—
                                the limiting—
                                the selecting—
                        of restricting options:
                                the options overlooked in youth,
                                the options bypassed in a livelihood,
                                the options unaccepted with maturity,
                                the options discarded by senility:
                                the options no longer present in a character.

    The options of freewill—
        the derivations of the catalysts which enhance a walk with God;
        the derivations of the catalysts which prevent a walk with God.

The end-time catalysts of destiny are:
                the commitment to the selected use of fusing choice;
                the ongoing postponement of such commitment;

- ANTHONY A EDDY (SCRIBE)

91

the denial of such commitment;
the abstracted absence of such commitment;
the onset of entry to the grave of man.

The end-time catalysts of destiny are recorded for the playing of the record back to man,
for the establishing of opportunities not taken up,
for the impingements on the spirit and the soul which has the insights shuffled off,
for the resonating sequences damped down at their birth,
for the recollection of all deposited in the waste bin of a life.

The waste bin of a life portrays the temptations as the trials foregone,
portrays the offerings as the rejections,
portrays the unaccepted in their fullness,
portrays the welcomed by deduction from the missing.

A destiny for man is certain and assured,
follows the reality of the grave as the soul awakes,
is crafted for the presence of the beings at the rising of The Son,
is determined as the catalysts are laid before the eyes and ears of man."

My Content Study Aid

_____

_____

_____

_____

_____

_____

_____

_____

_____

_____

_____

_____

_____

_____

_____

_____

_____

_____

The End-time Diet of My Sheep

"The diet of My sheep varies with the cultures in which they dwell,
        has a point of commonality
           which certifies the uniqueness of the flock when they feast
                in concert,
           which certifies The God of love upon a wind-blown slope
                when chewing all alone.

The diet of My sheep is attached to the physical and the spiritual,
           the secular and the sacred,
           the simplistic and the complex.

The diet of My sheep is a surfeit to the stomach and a surfeit to the soul,
           is a surfeit which arises from the keenness of My sheep,
                from the richness of the pasture,
                from the grazing made available.

The diet of My sheep cannot be robbed by the wolves which prowl,
           by the packs which circle,
           by a shepherd running free.

The diet of My sheep does not succumb to rotting,
           is not tainted by death,
           is not of the gall of bitterness.

The diet of My sheep is embellished by the latter rain,
           is upheld by the kingdom reign,
           is both varied and nourishing so growth can be retained.

The diet of My sheep has emphasis on the spiritual,
           spurns the secular in favour of the sacred,
           grazes in the waters of the word,
                in the paddocks of prayer,
                in the fields of tongues.

The diet of My sheep supplies muscles in the flesh,
           supplies marrow in the bones,
           supplies the fleeces of protection:
             clothing with the gifts of God,
             clothing with the armour of God,
             clothing with the sword of My Spirit in the mouth resting on
                the tongue,
             clothing with the sanctioning of the tongues by My Spirit.

The diet of My sheep leads them to know the battle cry of The Lord for 'He is risen—
                He is risen in deed.' "

- ANTHONY A EDDY (SCRIBE)

The End-time Prongs of Satan

"The prongs of Satan prod and push,
            stab and steer,
            lunge and tap.

The prongs of Satan discourage and dismay.
The prongs of Satan lie and cheat.
The prongs of Satan bend and cripple.

The prongs of Satan clout and bash,
            shake and threaten,
            tear and trip.

The prongs of Satan are the demons sowing discord in the life of man.

The prongs of Satan are the tripwires of disasters,
            are the delayers of decisions,
            are the dealers of disgust,
            are the dopers of destruction,
            are the charlatans of chance,
            are the vendors of the vanquished.

The prongs of Satan are the tacticians of the terrors,
            the naggers of the nightmares,
            the wrestlers of the woeful,
            the inviters of iniquity,
            the marshallers of manipulation,
            the testers of temptation.

The prongs of Satan are the besmirchers of the bashful,
            the gossipers of the group,
            the entanglers of the empires,
            the seekers of the surly,
            the ropers of the renegades,
            the violators of the victims.

The prongs of Satan are busy with the watchmen,
            are busy with the rearguards,
            are busy with the scouts.

The prongs of Satan are the spreaders of disease,
            the spreaders of malevolence,
            the specialists of pain.

The prongs of Satan are prepared to fight,
            do not like to lose,

carry grudges when defeated,
will return with more support,
struggle with an eviction.

The prongs of Satan are a nuisance to My people,
attempt to frustrate the will of God,
harry and bicker among themselves,
resist with lying tongues,
frighten the inept,
scare the lambs among the sheep.

The prongs of Satan are reluctant to leave when holding an invitation,
are reluctant to admit a presence,
are stupid in the things they say,
are vulnerable when their camouflage is lifted,
when the voice of God is present in His servants,
when the servants of God have the boldness,
with the wisdom,
to proceed unto completion:
with the vessel swept and cleaned."

My Content Study Aid

_____

_____

_____

_____

_____

_____

_____

_____

_____

_____

_____

_____

_____

_____

_____

_____

_____

The End-time Clouds of God

"The clouds of conquest build upon the efforts of the night which has no fear,
          display in majesty what has gone before,
          herald with perception a day of new beginnings.

The clouds of conquest are presented with the dawn,
          are presented with the keys,
          are presented for those who guard their souls.

The clouds of conquest are layered and substantial,
          are structured and with form,
          are grandiose and beautiful in the day of promise.

The clouds of conquest will shepherd and enfold,
          will welcome and position,
          will bring and carry forward.

The clouds of conquest magnify and glorify,
          transmit the music of the heavens,
          has a stage of splendour central and to the fore.

The clouds of conquest are the Hosts of Heaven enrobed in The Glory of The Kingdom.

The clouds of conquest dress the stage with the bands of light arrayed in all their colours:
          playing on the clouds of endearment.

The clouds of endearment dismiss the fear of heights,
    open in extension to bring The Love of God,
          The Promise of Sustaining,
          The Glory of The Heavens,
          The Majesty in Welcome,
    The Son Upon His Mission to claim His Bride in Waiting.

The clouds of endearment uplift all invited,
          easily support the gathering of The Beloved Within The Nations,
          of The People of The Lord,
          of The Endeared of God.

The clouds of endearment visit and transport,
          lower and secure,
          declare the Bride is Gathered with The Named intact.

The clouds of endearment are the loving angels from the nursery of God
          with their tasks fulfilled,
          with great joy in the outcomes,
          with great pleasure in the greeting of their charges:
          now no longer in their care."

The Garden of God

"The splendour of the garden is a vista laid out for the beloved to see.

The splendour of the garden is divided into three,
> has the scope of God,
> has the design of God,
> has the will of God,
>> in the indexed content,
>> in the beauty,
>> in the ease of access granted to the redeemed of God.

The splendour of the garden has vibrancy and life,
> has the inert as marvels,
> has the small,
> has the enormous,
>> each with its place to fill.

The splendour of the garden is never crowded,
> has freedom of movement without a hindrance to a thought,
> shows each to the best advantage with nothing pushed into
>> a corner.

The splendour of the garden has the flowers which never die,
>> never fade,
>> always make an impact on the senses.

The floral presentations contribute to the splendour of the garden,
> contribute to the beauty,
> contribute to the wonder due the gardener
>> in the garden of perfection,
>> in the garden for His children,
>> in the garden for His family:
>>> the family of God.

The splendour of the garden is beyond man in his mortality to comprehend the extent,
>> the attention to detail,
> all which is on display,
> all there for interaction,
> all there for the pleasure of the souls,
>> the joy of the spirits:
>> the presence of the new body of man—
>>> in his perfection and for his delight.

The splendour of the garden is not beset by night,
> has no footfalls of anxiety,
> has no sin within its threshold,

- ANTHONY A EDDY (SCRIBE)

has no cause for complaint,
has no seat of dissatisfaction,
    gives rise to no feelings of remorse.

The splendour of the garden has no time of man,
    has no cause to hurry,
    has no appointment to keep,
    has no source of stress.

The splendour of the garden carries nothing to measure the passage of time,
    has new concepts for guidance and instruction,
    visits the presence of God on all the many senses of man.

The splendour of the garden does not bequeath boredom to a soul,
    has much to take the interest,
    has much encouraging the closest of inspections,
    has much to impart afresh on each journey of discovery
            in The Garden of The Spirit,
            in The Garden of The Son,
            in The Garden of The Father.

The splendour of the garden has both the lion and the lamb at home within the fold
            of God."

My Content Study Aid

_____

_____

_____

_____

_____

_____

_____

_____

_____

_____

_____

_____

_____

_____

The End-time Foolishness of Man

"Is it not recorded in My word I hold creation in the palm of My hand?
Is it not recorded in My word of My mysteries hidden from man?
Is it not recorded in My word of My mastery of time?

Is it not yet possible for man to comprehend My law of cause and effect,
        when I dwell outside of time,
        when I triggered the 'big bang' as called by man from the contents
                of My hand,
        when I birthed the universe for man and started time upon
                his presence?

Foolish is he who strives to discard God into the waste bin stemming from
        man's knowledge.

Foolish is he who promotes his facts of God when lacking in experience,
        when remaining at a distance,
        when missing the building block of faith
          necessary for a commencement of a
          journey in the companionship of God.

Foolish is he who in his ignorance professed would destroy the walk of others in attacks
        upon their faith,
        does not evaluate the Spirit's giftings into the lives of others,
        has not been present in a setting where My Spirit is abounding.

Foolish is he who would decry the author of what is now before him as he reads,
        the past testimonies borne,
        the martyrs who surrendered all,
        the progress possible within the soul of man.

For wisdom would dictate reparation is difficult to establish in the sphere of loss of faith,
        of a resulting disjointed walk,
        of an indentured soul,
        of a damaged spirit queuing for a second death.

For these are the inheritance of the lost far in the world of intellect,
        imprisoned in their tower of ivory,
        where God is made unwelcome.

For foolish is the man who leads people from the truth,
        who inhibits faith in others,
        who shuts a door upon a scene of which he has no knowledge,
        who proclaims from afar that which he disdains to approach,
        who shouts in error and believes the echo,
        who manifests knowledge built upon a foolish heart.

- ANTHONY A EDDY (SCRIBE)

For such as these will be called to account for their actions as a fool,
    for their actions of destruction,
     for their impaling of the handiwork of God upon a picket where
           left to hang.

Beware the fool who transmits sincerity,
   who transmits nonsense wrapped in rotten fruit,
   who transmits his ignorance for the wise to see,
     for the wise to single out,
      for the wise to spread their wings to where
        the pasture is worth sampling.

Beware the fool living forever in the present,
   who does not lift his sight,
   who considers not his being,
   who settles for the dust,
   who chooses not to understand,
   who circumscribes a mountain with his wasted walk.

Beware the fool of business building a stack of hay on a foundation of wood and girded
          by the straw.

For such as they honour no-one but themselves,
   seek nothing but that which they can pocket,
   hold to nothing of end-time significance,
   are ill-prepared for what they will encounter,
   have no treasure set aside for a reigning day.

So it is the wise explore,
  the wise determine,
  the wise select,
  the wise walk the journey of reward,
   test the truth,
   discard the rumours,
   greet each day of promise.

So it is the wisdom of God is seen to rain upon their heads,
     to wash off the dust of Earth,
     to verify the Spirit's truth,
     to read the encountered way stations of The Lord.

So it is the wisdom of God brings discernment of all things,
    brings to understanding the mysteries of God in season,
    brings before each body-in-waiting
      the prospect of fulfilment as a temple,
      the equipping of the tongue,
      the commitment of the heart,
      the growth of faith in action."

The End-time Supremacy of Love

"Love overcomes all.

Love opens doors.

Love protects and caresses,
    uplifts and supports,
    cuddles and sustains,
    encourages and cheers.

Love sings the love song of the heart.

Love is reliable and trustworthy,
    is simple and direct,
    overlooks the slips,
    does not count the wayward steps,
    does not validate the lies,
    does not act the fool in matters of the spirit.

Love is full of joy,
    carries exuberance for the downcast,
    measures rations for the hungry,
    seeks healing for the injured and the hurting.

Love trusts within the word of wisdom not confounded by the word of knowledge.

Love shares the gifts of God,
        the providence of God,
        the testimonies of God,
        the companionship of God.

Love imparts the gift of tongues under the love of God.

Love shares the lives of sacrifice on a higher plane.

Love brings comfort to the uncomfortable,
    brings beauty to the ashes on a face,
    carries the miracles of God right up to the gates of Hell.

Love redeems the pledges of the penitent,
    restores the lonely and the impoverished,
    replaces the secular with the sacred.

Love varies little in its response,
    varies little in its approach,
    varies little in its reality of the day,
        in its reality of the night,
        in its reality of a relationship in time,

- ANTHONY A EDDY (SCRIBE)

in its relationship within eternity,
in its relationship between both God and man.

Love chastises without offence,
leaves the bonds intact,
draws from a storehouse of wealth which pays the price of all that is asked
without equivocation.

Love surfaces in the sea of doubt,
stirs the waves of splendour,
laps gently at the shoreline of honour and respect.

Love knows no boundaries of reproach immune from an apology,
knows no hindrances qualified to impair,
knows no shame that would cause a head to hang,
knows neither bitterness nor gall grow as the fruit of understanding.

Love cycles in the expressions of the heart,
in the expressions of the face,
in the expressions of the tongue,
in the expressions of the body,
in the expressions of the soul,
in the expressions of the spirit,
in the expressions of the tongues.

Love values life in all its beauty,
values the home of man in all its creativity,
values all the features of The Earth which give man cause to marvel at the wonders
placed before his eyes,
placed before his ears,
placed before his mouth,
placed before his nose,
placed before his feet,
placed before his reach:
all placed carefully in confirmation so man may come to know,
by awareness,
the very presence of his Loving God."

My Content Study Aid

_____

_____

_____

_____

_____

The End-time Wheels of Commerce

"The wheels of commerce rotate throughout The Earth,
        rotate in servicing the habitations of man,
        rotate in bringing the ordered across the distances,
        rotate in bearing the fruits of trade,
        rotate in meeting the needs and wants of man.

The wheels of commerce vary in velocity of transportation,
        vary in vulnerability to attack,
        vary in reliability in the weather,
        vary in circumstances of acceptance at the frontiers of man,
        vary in the makeup of the freight for destinations,
        vary in the demand by the recipients of orders.

The wheels of commerce load all they can carry,
        have few decisions of morality,
        see few calls upon the ethics of the enclaves which they serve.

The wheels of commerce vie with one another
        to meet the daybook of expenses,
        to haggle over the offered rate,
        to be the fastest to deliver,
        to repeat the gain as frequently as practical.

The wheels of commerce stop in places known to be inhospitable,
        in places caused by breakdowns,
        in places prepared for ambushes,
        in places where pillaging is witnessed,
        in places guards do not prevent the thefts,
        in places of scarcity of water,
        in places which oversee the trafficking in children stolen
                from their homelands.

The wheels of commerce are oiled from the oilcan squirting profit,
     from the greasing of the palms with tainted funds,
     from the smuggling of the undeclared without a trail of paper,
     from the transfer of the stolen embedded in disguise so the origin remains
                covered by the lie,
     from the deliveries to the warlords who value no life but their own,
     from the starving and the hungry when extortion plays its part with ruthlessness.

The wheels of commerce have no integrity of purpose when loaded up with lies to fill
                their tanks as fuel.

The wheels of commerce have no restitution where the dust of The Earth enters the
                nostrils of man.

- Anthony A Eddy (Scribe)

For as they breathe so death shall be serviced from The Earth.

The wheels of commerce have no recourse to grace or mercy when they ferry
          death into the hinterlands,
          death into the cities,
          death into the arms of man emboldened by freewill,
          death via the arms of man which stutter as they spew,
          death from the arms of man seen on the fields of slaughter.

The wheels of commerce should not be as a death-line,
          a harbinger of death,
          a courier of death:
      to the embattled who struggle against the invaders of known ferocity.
The wheels of commerce belie their name when dealing under a different flag.

The wheels of commerce are open to attack depending on the cargo being forwarded
                    for delivery.

The wheels of commerce should have no need for the circling of the caravans,
          for the issuing of either defensive or offensive orders,
          for fleeing in a chase from conquest.
The wheels of commerce should trade in peace,
        should encourage peace,
        should be introducing the value put on peace as development
                proceeds for the benefit of man.

The wheels of commerce are to benefit the lives of man
    with goods entrusted to that responsibility,
    with goods as known and viewed by God,
    with goods as originating from the knowledge pool of God for the benefit of man."

My Content Study Aid

_____

_____

_____

_____

_____

_____

_____

_____

_____

The End-time Wisdom

"Wisdom is not always knowledge-based,
>can sometimes be based on surroundings of the day,
>can be judged by circumstances,
>can be fed by experience,
>can be settled by a question,
>can be imparted from The Word,
>can be downloaded from God.

Wisdom accrues during man's mortality,
>is magnified in eternity,
>is imparted for the destiny of choice—
>>that within the family of God.

Wisdom is succinct and to the point,
>summarizes and extols,
>leaves little scope for the arguments of man,
>declares the thoughts of God revealed,
>always reflects the morality applicable to man.

Wisdom impacts on the ears of man,
>creates lasting impressions on the spirit and the soul,
>has content which is quotable and true,
>is for the long-term benefitting of the character of man,
>serves as an end-time sign of the involvement of God.

Wisdom cannot be purchased from God,
>remains under His will for a request for impartation,
>is measured for its value by the employing of its use in application.

Wisdom surfaces when the spirit is active,
>when the spirit has full participation,
>when the spirit is neither hampered nor hindered by the soul.

Wisdom evaporates in the presence of the fool,
>condenses in the presence of the wise,
>is significant in the presence of an assembly.

Wisdom is an infinite resource,
>is not limited to the mortality of man,
>can be accessed by the prayer of the spirit for the intent of the soul."

- ANTHONY A EDDY (SCRIBE)

The End-time Afflictions of Man

"The afflictions of man are many in number,
are many in effect.

The afflictions of man bring him to his knees in pain,
make him short of breath,
bring pain into his movements.

The afflictions of man affect his ability to move,
his ability to earn a living,
his ability to exercise his heart.

The afflictions of man are sometimes self-imposed,
are sometimes the results of habits becoming addictions of the day
and of the night.

The afflictions of man are often imposed at an opportunity of the foe of man.

The afflictions of man can be assigned by God,
can be dismissed by God,
can be assessed by God:
when man would test his God;
would curse his God;
would falsely testify of what his God has done.

The afflictions of God can be temporary or permanent within the mortality of man
depending upon the reaction of man
to the quest for which he seeks.

The afflictions of man can be corrective to his character:
can be evidence of his character,
can be the highlighting of his character,
can be displayed upon his face,
upon his limbs,
upon his body,
upon his hands and feet.

The afflictions of man can mimic the attributes of the spirit of man:
where a cramped spirit can lead to a cramped hand.

Such as these are evidence in the life of man of the result of the activities of the foe
of man—
unrestrained and free to roam to constrain the spirit,
the body or the soul.

The afflictions of man are not vested by God on the temples of God.

The temples of God suffer from the foe,

from the self,
when the hedge of protection is not erected,
pruned or fed.

The afflictions of man require perception to allocate the cause,
require a review of history,
a review of a walk,
a review of possible idolatry,
of possible instating by the foe of man,
of possible addictions by man imposed
upon himself.

The afflictions of man do not honour man;
arise from respect of his freewill;
arise as warning bells from God;
as attention getters from man himself—
as targeting from the foe of man as the prelude to
much worse.

The afflictions of man can be removed by God:
as such are sought from a change of heart,
as such are sought by the repelling of the foe of man,
as such are sought by understanding bringing a change in lifestyle—
where addictions cannot surface to appear within effective range
of the being of man.

The afflictions of man may not be pleasant to endure,
strengthen as they linger,
magnify the weakness,
enhance a disability,
sing a song of mourning for that which has been lost.

The afflictions of man are best dealt with at the onset—
when a muscle cramps,
when a muscle twitches,
when a muscle is defiant to instructions.

The afflictions of man are best dealt with when first attaining sufficient severity to
become the centre of attention.

The afflictions of man react to prayer and fasting,
react to anointing,
react to the hands of healing.

The afflictions of man react to the attentive care of man and the cause thereof.

The afflictions of man can be but a sneeze,
or a cough which lingers in locations known to comfort so
to nurture.

- ANTHONY A EDDY (SCRIBE)

107

The afflictions of man can be suffered by man,
or dispensed with by man,
depending on his freewill linking—
to both his knowledge and his wisdom.

The afflictions of man are under the oversight of God."

My Content Study Aid

_____

_____

_____

_____

_____

_____

_____

_____

_____

_____

_____

_____

_____

_____

_____

_____

_____

_____

_____

_____

_____

_____

_____

_____

_____

_____

The End-time Vitality of A Nation

"The vitality of a nation depends on its understanding,
on its wisdom,
both professed and displayed,
on its vision for the future based both on peace and the
well-being of its peoples.

The vitality of a nation depends on its relationship with its neighbours,
on its righteousness of rule,
on its perception of the truth.

The vitality of a nation depends on the sanctity afforded life,
the value put on families,
the education of the young.

The vitality of a nation depends on its belief in justice,
its enforcement agencies forsaking violence and
beyond the control of despots wearing
sneers with lies upon their lips.

The vitality of a nation is dependent on productivity;
a workforce who is willing;
a judiciary who does not know corruption;
an ombudsman who is alert and articulate,
who has an open door which leads to accountability.

The vitality of a nation should highly value friendship,
highly value freedom,
highly value The God of Revelation—
The God who lives and loves and who knows The Lion which roars.

The vitality of a nation should swing the trade doors open,
should spread the welcome mat to those who drive the caravans,
should seal the typed documents in honour so the typing can be
seen in action.

The vitality of a nation cannot long survive in isolation,
cannot long survive with guns along a frontier,
cannot long survive where the powerful and the rich place their
gold in foreign banks of secrecy.

The vitality of a nation flourishes where flowers are valued for their beauty,
where cleanliness speaks volumes to the visitors,
where truth can be shouted from the rooftops,
where the laws are passed by the agreement of
the people,

- ANTHONY A EDDY (SCRIBE)

where there is the fear of God abroad and His favour is
well known.

The vitality of a nation speaks of a happy nation,
a joy filled nation,
a righteous nation—
where there is no fear of man and each attends his neighbour as himself."

My Content Study Aid

_____

_____

_____

_____

_____

_____

_____

_____

_____

_____

_____

_____

_____

_____

_____

_____

_____

_____

_____

_____

_____

_____

_____

The End-time Pestering of Man

"The pestering of man is persistent and ongoing,
        is carried out by those of lower ilk than demons—
    the imps within the shadows who both tempt and tease,
        who both annoy and return,
        who both test for an open door and an invitation.

The pestering of man is specific and precise,
        is nasty and consistent,
        is ominous and threatening.

The pestering of man discovers his access points of vulnerability,
        those with his objections,
        those with his acceptance.

The pestering of man builds on the presence of his lies,
        on the presence of deceit,
        on the presence of unrighteousness within the heart
        and soul.

The pestering of man inoculates the body and the soul as if a mosquito sucking blood,
        as if a touch too light to feel,
        as if an input not considered
        sufficient to sound a
        warning note to man.

The pestering of man explores the possibilities of leading him to shame,
        to secreting in the cave of privacy,
        to entering the twilight zone with the approach
        of darkness.

The pestering of man should be realized for what it is,
        should be stopped from developing further,
        should be prevented from being listed as a target—
        as a target for attack.

The pestering of man cannot penetrate the mantle of The Spirit,
        the covering of God,
        the presence of a temple.

The pestering of man is offered his protection,
        his means of circumventing his foe in action,
        his assurance that pestering will be of no effect.

The pestering of man is not a sign of God,
        is not a sign of benefit to man,
        is not a sign leading to good health.

- ANTHONY A EDDY (SCRIBE)

The pestering of man is a sign of the need for grace,
of the need for My Spirit's presence,
of the need for a new covenant in force.

The pestering of man is at variance with the will of God."

My Content Study Aid

_____
_____
_____
_____
_____
_____
_____
_____
_____
_____
_____
_____
_____
_____
_____
_____
_____
_____
_____
_____
_____
_____
_____
_____
_____
_____

The End-time Buzzing of The Bees

"The buzzing of the bees indicates the health of the colony,
the size of the colony,
the activity of the colony.

The buzzing of the bees speaks of warmth and sunshine,
speaks of flowers and nectar,
speaks of many journeys storing each bee's prize—
each bee's labour—
each bee's contribution to the hive.

The buzzing of the bees is the backdrop signing health in the environment,
health in pollination,
health in expectation of a crop of man.

The buzzing of the bees can be a swarm at large,
can be a swarm out searching,
can be a swarm awaiting reports of a new location,
can be a swarm leaving cramped conditions for the open spaces,
can be a swarm committed to a flight.

The buzzing of the bees can be silenced by smoke,
can be silenced by sprays,
can be silenced by destruction of the hive.

The buzzing of the bees can be heard in a tree in blossom,
on a field of flowers,
in the proximity of a vibrant hive.

The buzzing of the bees is as a school of children set free into a playground,
is as a stream seen rushing past the rocks,
is as a distant chainsaw heard felling all the trees,
is as the hum of traffic packed upon a motorway,
is as the racing of the engines for peak speed upon a racetrack.

The buzzing of the bees is not heard in the rain,
is not heard in the night,
is not heard in the wind storm of ferocity,
is not heard when the lights are red,
is not heard by an upraised hand,
is not heard in the presence of construction.

The buzzing of the bees should be a welcome sound to man,
is a welcome sound to God,
is an indicator to God of the health of His creation,
is a sign of the interactivity of His creation as it follows the quest for life."

- ANTHONY A EDDY (SCRIBE)

The End-time Squirrels of The Earth

"The squirrels love their habitats,
    adjust to their habitats,
    secrete and put aside in a time of plenty,
    have a storehouse in reserve when the need is evident,
    scamper in busyness when surplus is to the fore.

The squirrels of The Earth have lessons there for man:
       do not contaminate that which serves a future dependency,
       guard the living space from invasion,
       shelter and protect the family from the ravages of storms,
       gather while one may—
  for as the lean times approach so the will is tested,
         so the character is stressed,
         so the soul knows invitations where sinning
            is encouraged.

The squirrels do not risk survival with a single depository;
    spread their forward survival items where others will neither discover
           nor uplift;
    ensure there is a surplus to their needs so starvation is held at bay;
    know to store them where they are not pillaged,
       where they are not subject to decay,
       where they are held for when appetites demand.

The squirrels come and go,
    attend and prosper,
    know and understand:
       within the vagaries encountered.

The squirrels thrive and multiply,
    experience and replenish,
    read and prepare:
       for the cycle of restoration.

The squirrels scamper and enjoy the fruits in season,
    select and save the kernels of delight,
    explore and discover the bounty set upon their table by The Loving God.

The Loving God who sees each sparrow fall;
    who puts His imprimatur upon each life within creation;
    who has a headdress waiting for each created in His image;
    who calls each to begin,
       to complete,
       the freewill journey home—

as He holds each place prepared,
     each inheritance to be shared,
     each welcome kept in readiness."

My Content Study Aid

_____

_____

_____

_____

_____

_____

_____

_____

_____

_____

_____

_____

_____

_____

_____

_____

_____

_____

_____

_____

_____

_____

_____

_____

_____

_____

_____

- ANTHONY A EDDY (SCRIBE)

The End-time Bowing of The Seas

"The bowing of the seas measures the tranquility of God.

The bowing of the seas arises from the winds of the four corners of The Earth.

The bowing of the seas can be a maelstrom in the making,
        can test the constructions of man,
        can expose a ship caught within its storm.

The bowing of the seas beats upon the shorelines,
        batters all forms of constraint,
        surges and recedes with a will as if its own.

The bowing of the seas can be peaceful and gentle,
        can rest within the billows coloured with the evening,
        can water a cupped hand in cooling from the heat,
        can inundate the diver searching for a meal,
        can lead and mix the currents of the outreaches from the
                distant lands,
        can carry the flecks of foam from where they have been birthed.

The bowing of the seas replenishes their capacity for life for all who dwell therein:
        cleanse and purify the contaminants dumped by man;
        carry and disperse the concentrates of man;
        acts as a repository for the discards of man;
        yields its pleasures to the recreation of man;
        poses the challenges of distances for the conquest of man.

The bowing of the seas presents its wealth to man,
        churns the food of nations,
        surrenders from its depths the valued which man describes
                as precious,
        invites the exploration of the ignorance of man,
        witnesses the surrender of that buried in its beds,
        overcomes the thoughtless who set forth unprepared.

The bowing of the seas is a wonder to behold in the eyes of man:
        is at rest under clear blue skies with lapping to the fore,
        is at its heights of majesty where the wind force is unchecked.

The bowing of the seas propels and drags,
        submerges and uplifts,
        buries and surrenders.

The bowing of the seas merge with the colours of the day,
        the intensity of luminosity under conditions of enhancement,
        the sparkling on the scintillations of the jewel drops of the sea.

The bowing of the seas acknowledges the lady of the night who strains and grasps,
                    who relinquishes a hold—
                              yet to seize again,
                    who stores up and releases the surges known to man,
                    who brings the shimmering reflections of much beauty,
                    who feeds the eyes of man when the shades are drawn,
                    who times her entrance and her exit:
                                        to the retreat—
                                        to the influx—
                                        of the lighting of the day.

The bowing of the seas is correctly ascribed to the majesty of God,
                    is beyond the controls of man,
                    expresses might and power under authority,
                    demonstrates the control of God.

        Foolish are they who go adventuring into the face of God without protection.

        Wise are they who are seen to travel in the fear of God."

My Content Study Aid

_____
_____
_____
_____
_____
_____
_____
_____
_____
_____
_____
_____
_____
_____
_____
_____
_____
_____

The End-time Whitebait of The Seas

"The whitebait of the seas is a delicacy to the palate of man.

The whitebait of the seas spawn up the rivers on a rising tide,
     seek the reeds,
     progress the cycle which preserves their being.

The whitebait of the seas travel in their shoals.
     are netted in their shoals,
     are vanquished in their shoals.

The whitebait of the seas are pressured by the catch of man,
     are pressured by the value ascribed by man,
     are pressured by diminishing resources within the tidal reach.

The whitebait of the seas battle the ebb and flow in the presence of rapacious feeders,
     run the gauntlet of the river banks where the current weakens,
     seek the clearest waters when mud has not contaminated.

The whitebait of the seas cannot sustain their harvesting—
     in the season set for placing eggs upon the reeds where the
          tide has reach.

The whitebait of the seas are not a necessary adjunct to the diet of man.

The whitebait of the seas are not essential to be battered on the platters of the rich
          and careless,
    do not deserve to be stripped and weighed for the naming by the few
          accustomed to their luxury,
    do not deserve to be driven to extinction by the greed and tastelessness
          of man,
    do not deserve to have their way of life mopped up by the few for
         serving up to the unappreciative:
   of the beauty of the functioning of what is being placed within their mouths.

So the few constrain the many,
   so the few restrict rebirth,
   so the few harvest for the purse,
   so the few pursue the remnants—
    of that once used to fertilize the gardens near the river mouths.

So the few boast of their endeavours,
    take all that they can catch,
    seize upon the chance to wrest the very last as some struggle to avoid the nets.

So the shoals,
   still not seen as a misnomer,

mostly come in threes and fours as individuals are counted on the fingers of
one hand,
still do not dishearten those addicted to their capture.

Yet still the garners of the riverbanks wait in expectation of a haul,
in the daylight hours when the tide is on the rise,
in the quest for profit from which used to be a hobby.

So is destroyed the inheritance of a nation:
as the proceeds of the raping of the river banks is squandered on the frivolous;
that which exists nowhere else on Earth;
that which is not invested in the future;
that which has to dredge up memories of how it once appeared for the
benefit of man.

Oh that the greed of man could be tempered by supply,
could be tempered with replenishment,
could be tempered by conserving,
could be tempered by the wisdom necessary to know when enough
suffices in the land of plenty.

The land of plenty—
placed in the distant seas,
where penguins paddle to attend their nests,
where the dolphins frolic in enjoyment,
where the seals breed in peace upon the rocks,
where the whales display their majesty to visitors from afar,
where the seabirds with their wingspans soar—
to carry their pickings to the open mouths.

So the big and powerful grab attention while the midgets succumb to ravishing—
in the twilight of their being away from the supervision of the visitors."

My Content Study Aid

_____

_____

_____

_____

_____

_____

_____

_____

- ANTHONY A EDDY (SCRIBE)

The End-time Shouting of Man

"The shouting of man while confined to his crib is less than a spasm in eternity,
                                        is less than a twinkle of a star,
                                        is less than a flash of lightning in the
                                                    absence of the thunder.

The shouting of man tires out the eardrums when heard to completion,
                    tires out the eardrums while composing a reply,
                    tires out the eardrums when repeated until exhausted by the passage
                                                                of time.

The shouting of man should not be on a timetable,
                    should not be born of inexperience,
                    should not carry a message of unimportance.

The shouting of man comes to be ignored by the wise,
                    always surprises the fool,
                    tends to be short of apologies deserved,
                    encourages like raising of voices as if appearing on a stage.

The shouting of man is amplified by man,
                    is flung into the void with an echo tumbling after,
                    loses its crispness of delivery in excessive distortion which muddies
                                                                up the message.

The shouting of man is ineffective when the objective is to transfer knowledge,
                    serves very little purpose when met by an opposing shout,
                    is lost in the uproar when joined by several others.

The shouting of man is ill-considered at the best,
                                        is worthless at the worst;
                    achieves very little at the best,
                                        is useless at the worst;
                    is overbearing at the best,
                                        is ignored at the worst.

The shouting of man wears the eardrums out before the day completes,
                    needs the muffs in place so distractions cannot penetrate,
                    gives venting of the anger from arousal at the petty and remote.

The shouting of man signs of patience exhausted,
                        of frustration in full flow,
                        of anger released where control is very shallow,
                        of a will not able to dominate an exchange,
                        of a freewill choice to misbehave without recourse,
                        of an intent to bully so to prevail,

of the option to make an opinion heard,
to impinge on a discussion where nothing is contributed.

The shouting of man signs of reaching across a distance when attention is avidly sought.

The shouting of man diminishes his stature,
is not encountered in the presence of a king,
should not be encountered by a king in-waiting,
should not be used by a king in-waiting.

The shouting of man should be restricted to a warning at the imperilment of life,
should be restricted to a greeting where the voice needs to carry,
should be restricted to a search where the lost need to be found,
should be restricted to when addressing a gathering of listeners.

The shouting of man is not intended for confrontation of a class,
is not intended to coerce a child,
is not intended to intimidate an individual,
is not intended to broadcast blasphemy across the lips of man.

The shouting of man should not be a last-ditch effort to get the attention of God.

The shouting of man precludes a close relationship with God,
precludes the fear of God,
precludes a message reaching the very ears of God as the
angels scatter."

My Content Study Aid

_____

_____

_____

_____

_____

_____

_____

_____

_____

_____

_____

_____

_____

- ANTHONY A EDDY (SCRIBE)

The End-time Volleyball of Man

"The volleyball of man is tossed around by man,
        is tossed to and fro—
                that which no-one seeks to catch,
                that which no-one seeks to pickup,
                that which seems to be best passed on to another.

The volleyball of man is as the thorns baked on the crust of bread,
        is as the poison floating on the wine,
        is as the shadow of death seen spread across the river of life.

The volleyball of man passes the strife unto another,
        sees the contaminants flow through the sieves of purity,
        witnesses the falling of the hail on the crops of tenderness.

The volleyball of man tracks as a wrecking ball trailed in the mud,
        as a burst of colour seeping down a watercolour,
        as dirty ice found melting on the pristine snow,
        as the blood of man found soaking into The Earth.

The volleyball of man succumbs to responsibility exercised,
        succumbs to righteousness endowed,
        succumbs to accountability examined,
        succumbs to the fear of God.

The volleyball of man is as a snowball rolling down a hill;
        gathers mass and speed as it progresses to its end;
        bursts upon a scene of chaos mixed with disrepute;
        renders mayhem to the fore and aft,
            to the left and right,
            to the up and down.

The volleyball of man is as a time bomb in a capsule,
        is as that sealed in a tin upon a fire,
        is as that screwed in a glass exposed to the hottest of hot water,
        is as that which bursts unexpectedly upon a scene where it has
                        no home.

The volleyball of man speaks of a flawed character—
                not properly developed,
                not critically examined,
                not pensively explored.

The volleyball of man speaks of a temper only partially controlled,
        of emotions not far from their flash points,
        of the idols all inviting the attentions of frustration,

of the love of money with all its related hangers-on.

The volleyball of man bounces to the detriment of man in the winds of lethargy;
bounces to the detriment of man in gathering the losses,
in shedding the gains;
bounces to the detriment of man in the casino brought to life—
which favours the other rather than the one.

The volleyball of man bounces to the detriment of man both in fairness and in fame,
both in companionship and
in solitude,
both in wealth and in happiness:
when the volleyball of man crosses the line beyond which God
chooses not to honour the freewill of man."

My Content Study Aid

_____

_____

_____

_____

_____

_____

_____

_____

_____

_____

_____

_____

_____

_____

_____

_____

_____

_____

_____

_____

_____

The End-time Voice in The Wilderness

"The voice in the wilderness is difficult to distinguish from the noise of man;
is difficult to discern in its existence;
is difficult to comprehend the message
when uttered from afar,
when not heralded clearly,
when falling on inattentive ears.

The voice in the wilderness can proclaim a message of great import,
a message for considering,
a message bringing change,
a message in affirmation of the will of God.

The voice in the wilderness can carry round the globe,
can carry across the waters,
can carry across the lands of man,
can affect the way that man does live and dwell.

The voice in the wilderness can bring insights of great value:
can reinforce in strengthening the past into the present,
can verify the integrity of the happenings of the day,
can present a scenario portraying the end-time despoliation of
the habitat of man.

The voice in the wilderness can awaken the sleepers and the slumberers:
to that which passes by unnoticed when driven by the busy and
the thoughtless,
the greedy and the gatherers,
the selfish and the grabbers,
the thieves and the varlets,
the hoarders and the storers—
all those with an interest in the price hikes imposed upon the back
of scarcity—
scarcity arching in the spasms born of contrived shortages in supply.

The voice in the wilderness often speaks of what others miss,
often trumpets folly in the making,
often highlights those who see themselves as unaccountable
to their fellow man.

The voice in the wilderness often speaks with wisdom,
often speaks with insights of the future if the ways of man
continue as they are,
often speaks in fear of retribution if the message is
unpalatable and the addressees are well-seated.

The voice in the wilderness can be easily silenced

in the amphitheatre born of ridicule,

in the amphitheatre born of disqualifying by mixing in
the unacceptable,

in the amphitheatre born of attribution to the misfits and
the incoherent—

so cogency is lost as truth is flayed upon the whipping post of lies.

For by such means can the message be ignored;

can the message be immersed in nonsense before understanding
is attained;

can the message intended for the coming dawn be silenced in
the night;

can the heralds,

without temerity,

become convinced:

the opportunity to broadcast what they know to
be of value is not in their own self-interests.

So the audience is denied a recounting—

by the publicists of the night and the cautious of the day.

The voice in the wilderness can be the voice of self-aggrandizement of the aggrieved
of man;

can be the voice of Satan in his hostility of bitterness using man for his
mimicking of God;

can be the voice of God through His prophets whom He knows:

can be either the voice of destruction aimed at man by Satan—

or the voice of life within eternity offered to man by his God in all His
glory of creation.

For such are the days within which man now lives.

For such are the end-time days of which man has been warned.

For such are the days in which the prophets of God are commissioned so to speak the
will of God in declaration—

as the voice of God has been heard by His prophets whom He knows:

with certainty,

with the absence of error,

in recalling the scriptures of God—

those destined to guide and counsel man with knowledge and with wisdom—

as man within the flock of God prepares to receive The Living Christ
returning for His Bride."

Scribal Note*:*

The Bible, (New King James version)

Isaiah 40:3

- ANTHONY A EDDY (SCRIBE)

The voice of one crying in the wilderness:
> "Prepare the way of the LORD;
> Make straight in the desert
> A highway for our God.

Matthew 3:3,
> For this is he who was spoken of by the prophet Isaiah, saying:
> > "The voice of one crying in the wilderness:
> > Prepare the way of the LORD;
> > 'Make His paths straight.'"

My Content Study Aid

_____

_____

_____

_____

_____

_____

_____

_____

_____

_____

_____

_____

_____

_____

_____

_____

_____

_____

_____

_____

_____

The End-time Queries on Aspects of Revival

Scribal Notes:

A. *This item was initially personal in its presentation. Here it is laid out for general perusal which requires incidental very minor changes for dictated clarity of what was assumptive content containing pronouns and names. (e.g 'it' referring to the noun.) The original personal item exists if required for validation by comparison. This generalised item is approved by The Lord for release.*

B. *'And I hear the Lord Jesus saying,' should be taken as a preface to each response which follows in quotation marks— " ".*

Scribal initiated queries are in numbered bold italicised texts for ease of locating.

1. What I am interested in, is that particular aspect of Your discipling, Lord, which gives rise to, and so brings about, Revival in one of Your churches?

"Revival is encouraged by My people in passing through the courts of praise and
of worship,
past the rented curtain,
into the holy of holies,
and there not be adjudged trespassers without the right of entry,
but as supplicants to The God of Abraham."

2. It seems so hard to ignite the fire, Lord, as if everyone is using damp or, worse, wet kindling, which won't catch the fire, or can't catch the fire.

"The fire can not be lit by the lone efforts of man.

The fire is lit from The Flame of My Spirit,
within the unity of God,
when all is well within My church,
when My leadership are in accord—
when My leadership are active in their taskings—
when My leadership all know the fear of God—
when My people are seeking meat between their teeth rather than
milk upon their tongues—
when My people come to understand and to seek
that which is not present in their lives:
that which could be and yet is not.

My people need to be familiar with the keys of the kingdom and practised in their use.
My people need to be familiar with My Spirit's gifts and practised in their use.
My people need to be attuned to the will of God and confident in its discernment.
My people need to be welcoming of My Spirit and accepting of His counsel.
My people need to be attentive to The Living God who has spoken with the patriarchs
and knows the forbears and the martyrs of the faith."

- ANTHONY A EDDY (SCRIBE)

3. I don't know how the fire is started, my Lord.

"The fire falls when unity of purpose of My leadership is evident,

of prayer which requests the fire,

of tongues which know the fire,

of intensity of passion for that Revival which others
have sought and gained,

of action built upon the heart's intent,

of sincerity of expression,

of righteousness of character,

of perseverance of the soul:

in order to prevail to continue past the season—

which sees the bored and the disenchanted no longer attend their calls,

which sees the 'Holy Spirit' seekers departing to the foot of yet
another 'holy' mountain,

which sees the lukewarm lose commitment and so forsake their vows.

The fire falls where freedom reigns,

where My Spirit testifies of being welcome,

where the wise know to wait upon The Lord,

where holiness is not impeded from descending,

where the fear of God pervades,

where the denseness of the fog of sin no longer clings,

no longer envelops,

no longer keeps its captives,

with their then residues in tow,

in pre-emption of a relationship with The God of reconciliation."

3a. Or how it is to be nurtured so it continues to burn indefinitely.

"The fire is fuelled both by repentance and by gratitude.

As these increase so the fire burns more brightly—

so the fire becomes as a furnace,

as the Refiner's fire,

in dealing with the dross.

As these decrease so the fire begins to fade—

becoming as a glimmer,

where the embers barely glow,

on the pathway to extinction."

4. It seems like the people suffer burn out through exhaustion, Lord, after a very intense but relatively short time where Revival is evident and glory everywhere abounding?

"Revival requires an on-going source of fuel if it is to continue and more so if it is
to expand.

The diminution of a Revival is not due to the 'exhaustion' of those within the church, but rather the exhaustion of fresh fuel in the locality of its birth.

Revival comes intended to be as a rolling thunder which moves across a landscape,
which travels progressively through the
churches and their surrounds,
which behaves as if a set of dominoes
which trickle according to the setting,
according to the turns and
twists built into that
laid out for attention.

My church is yet to acquire the wisdom and the understanding enabling the passing of the
baton of Revival to each church in turn—
prior to the church of bequeathal having embers which only dully glow,
where the flames are scarcely visible,
where the heat barely attains the status of being regarded as lukewarm.

For then the baton of the flame is no longer incandescent and struggles to maintain
the firebrand needed to build a fresh Refiner's fire—
as the dominoes fall while the hopeful and expectant wait:
for the flashpoint of ignition which may be long delayed."

5. Is there a progressive path towards Revival?

"Yes.
Revival is intended to roll across the countryside;
to jump the waters of the deep;
to visit both the ice and marsh,
both the snow and desert,
both the swamp and high places,
both the cob hut and the castle."

5a. Or is it Your sovereign act of blessing?

"Yes.
Revival is a sovereign act of blessing;
is a sovereign act of selection;
is a sovereign act within the sweep of time.

Revival is stationed for installing when My Spirit reports that all is well within a
gathering of My people:
they who are yearning for the signature of their faith."

5b. Or is it still to remain a mystery of God?

"As Revival has been already declared and experienced by man so it no longer is held as
a mystery of God;
rather,
it is held close to the heart of God for the end-time preparation of those in need
of repentance with the fall of grace—
for the multitudes at large who would encounter God."

- ANTHONY A EDDY (SCRIBE)

5c. *Do you speak to Your prophets concerning the onset of Revival?*

"As the queries of My prophets are received,
    so the responses are revealed.
As the queries are expanded,
    so the responses are extended."

6. *Is there something You expect from us, Your people, which is missing and so disqualifies us from participation?*

"Yes.

The missing 'something' is difficult but not impossible for man to achieve.

This 'something' is often that which causes My church to stumble.

Understanding should bring My church to its knees.

That 'something' is not often sought as counsel from My Spirit:
    of how it may be achieved,
    of how it may be embedded in a flock,
    of how it may be strongly valued as a mainstay of My church.

The God of Love requires His church to be as one in unity:
    in all aspects of relationship,
        of discipling,
        of fellowship,
        of effort and of will.

As The Father The Son and The Holy Spirit are one in unity,
    so the bride of Christ is expected so to be
        within their gowns of spotless white.

Disunity is not of God,
    is evaluated as sin:
        as it fragments and distorts,
        as it separates—
        generating huddles on the sidelines where whispers are the order,
            where grievances are aired as
                support is garnered from
                among the dirt and filth.

So the leadership of My church is dishonoured by the actions of the sheep within
                their care—
        who impugn their integrity so piousness and
            piety are both robbed of their reward."

7. *Lord, You know our hearts. Is there another term we should be using?*

"The intent of every heart is known to God,
        regardless of how man chooses to encode either his deeds or his tongue—
            in the language of the day."

8. How do we qualify, Lord, to be immersed within a Revival brought by You, Lord?

"To advance in unity and so be heard as supplicants and not as interlopers."

9. Can a Revival be centred in Your Church under Your Pastors here in Hamilton, New Zealand, Lord, or, indeed, wherever one of Your worldwide churches happens to be located?

"Where My Spirit is welcomed in unity and free to move,
                    the whole gamut of God is available for the experiencing by man."

10. Supplementary How is the baton passed, Lord, so the dominoes continue to fall and the Revival flourishes in each new location?

"So the bottom line is reached;
  so the questions have been sorted;
  so the answer is desired by the attentive and the earnest;
  so the baton of revival is revealed to those lacking the knowledge inherent for
                                                            its passing.

The baton of Revival is as a bus waiting at a bus stop waiting for the travellers.

The baton of Revival moves the intent of My Spirit prior to the lack of fuel:
            to where the fuel is seen to gather with My people and is plentiful in scope.

The baton of Revival seizes the end-time day with power,
                              with authority,
                              with My Spirit leading with His flame
                                            borne high:
                                    to toss aside the henchmen of the devil;
                                    to so hear man testify of Me.

The baton of Revival is the end-time signature of God.

    Woe to those who attempt to interfere with the signature of God.
    Woe to those who do not support the signature of God.
    Woe to those who cut and flee before the signature of God.

    Blessed are those reborn under the baton of revival.

    Blessed are those restored under the baton of revival.

    Blessed are those revived who hold fast to their vows,
                        who resolve to keep their promises,
                        who hold to their commitments:
                                    the sacred trusts instated by the baton of revival.

    Blessed are those who enter into My Kingdom,
                        who value the fall of grace,
                        who hold fast to the sacraments of the sacrifice,
                        who honour the new covenant both in its aspects and intent.

    Blessed are those who would emulate My disciples of the past,

- ANTHONY A EDDY (SCRIBE)

131

who would follow Me in the bounds of discipleship,
who would follow Me as willing servants with love for their
fellow man.

The baton of Revival installs the outflow of My Spirit active and ready—
for a new beginning at a more distant location.

The baton of Revival lays afresh the fire to embrace the new fuel for the stoking of
the fire.

The baton of Revival brings the spreading of the fire of God in the busloads of
My people—
selected from those who had previously just travelled through the refining fire,
with a testimony to bear before those at a fresh location:
those who would follow them into a time to
be spent with their living God made known.

Thus it is the 'on fire' servants of The Living God who
carry so to light the kindling fuel afresh,
see it flare and catch,
see it spread and evolve,
see the feast of miracles and wonders appearing in the gatherings of man,
see the growth and power of testimonies born within the witnesses,
born within the penitents,
born within the fall of grace,
born within the heart of man.

So families of rebirth enter into unity,
are filled with a common goal in reaching out within the
end-time faith.

The baton of Revival is the end-time servants of God,
presentable and well,
fit and refreshed,
with hands afire in readiness for laying on,
with the gifting and the emboldenment
arising from The Holy Spirit—
as God attends His Earthly kingdom for the glory of The Son.

The baton of Revival sees the busloads departing for new sites:
under the auspices of God to reclaim the souls for God;
both numerous and sufficient to overcome any reluctance encountered;
to stay to oversee through the days of introduction until the fire is
thoroughly ignited;
as the fire of God becomes capable of absorbing all the fuel which
comes to yield to God.

So the baton of Revival continues on to fresh areas in the will of God and the
enthusiasm of My end-time people to set The Earth on fire."

The End-time Fall of Grace

"The fall of grace is wide and varied:
    is as if scattered by the wind of Heaven,
    is as if contained within each drop of rain,
    is prepared in full abundance for the end-time need of man.

The fall of grace is silent yet speaks to the spirit of man.
The fall of grace is real yet cannot be touched by man.
The fall of grace reconciles man yet cannot be bought or sold.

The fall of grace envelops man in his completeness:
    envelops man in his sin,
    envelops man through his repentance,
    envelops man for a new beginning,
    envelops man with the reality of God,
    envelops man as fitted-out for eternity,
    envelops man in a call of preparation as His bride.

The fall of grace humbles the weak and the mighty,
    humbles the lonely and the family,
    humbles the reticent and the brash,
    humbles the ignorant and the wise,
    humbles the seeker and the satisfied,
    humbles the destitute and the wealthy,
    humbles the agnostic and the atheist.

The fall of grace brings all before the throne of grace,
    leads all to the sacrifice of grace,
    teaches from the past into the present unto the future.

The fall of grace is not determined by the amount of sin:
        by the type of sin,
        by the proximity of sin,
        by the adoption of sin,
        by the effect of sin,
        by the length of sin,
        by the promises of sin.

The fall of grace transmits the forgiveness of God,
        the acceptance by God,
        the adoption into the family of God.

The fall of grace transmits the cleansing power of God,
    installs a new guest in the framework of the house,
    opens up the access to the bounty of God,

- ANTHONY A EDDY (SCRIBE)

marks a fresh relationship with God,
initiates the giftings of His Spirit.

The fall of grace justifies man in the sight of God:
in man's new beginning,
in man's discarding of the past,
in man's refurbishment of his life,
in man's reorientation of the values fit for aspirations,
in man's re-evaluation of the sacred and the holy.

The fall of grace changes friends and enemies,
brings understanding of the changes,
introduces arming and equipping from the armoury of God.

The fall of grace leads to righteousness and to peace.

The fall of grace rewards the commitment of man's spirit:
qualifies for the promises of God,
changes attitudes to all that went before,
strengthens the will of man to become an overcomer,
opens new visions with their vistas for attainment by the soul.

The fall of grace is a turning point in the life of man,
in the mortality of man,
in the judgment of man.

The fall of grace opens up a safe harbour of great beauty where the soul and the spirit
may be endowed by God."

My Content Study Aid

_____
_____
_____
_____
_____
_____
_____
_____
_____
_____
_____
_____

The End-time Circumcision of The Heart

"The circumcision of man should no longer involve the genitals of man.

The end-time circumcision of man speaks:
> of the circumcision of the heart—
>> the freeing it from sin,
>> the cleaning of the chambers,
>> the clearing of the dungeons,
>> the cleansing of the rooms.

The end-time circumcision of man speaks:
> of the effective prayer needs of the heart—
>> the sincerity of the intent of the heart,
>> the purity of the heart,
>> the unity of the heart,
>> the faithfulness of the beat.

The end-time circumcision of the heart
> addresses outstanding rites and wrongs,
> addresses carried sin still burdening,
> addresses unforgiven trespasses still awaiting action,
> addresses thoughts of fancy surfacing from the soul,
> addresses matters of the will in conflict with the spirit.

The end-time circumcision of the heart corrects the imbalance of man,
> corrects his tendency to lean,
> corrects his ability to stand upright.

The end-time circumcision of the heart removes the sticky sins
> of influence,
> of past wrongs wrought,
> of present influences noted for their undesirability:
> those which are to have no presence in the bride of Christ.

The end-time circumcision of the heart admits the secondment of unity,
> dismisses disarray,
> welcomes the steadfast and the sure.

The end-time circumcision of the heart is the precursor of good health,
> the harbinger of righteousness,
> the dry-cleaner of each wardrobe's robes and
>> gowns on display unto The Lamb.

The end-time circumcision of the heart appeals in purity to the angels,
> justifies an empty slate,
> expunges all the records' built-in history requiring expurgation.

- ANTHONY A EDDY (SCRIBE)

The end-time circumcision of the heart is the process of procession,
              is the activity awaited,
              is the birthright of the bride in seeking purity
                    of thought—
                         with word—
                         with deed.

The end-time circumcision of the heart impales sin upon the cross,
                    consigns sin to darkness where it rightfully belongs,
                    separates sin from within the presence of the bride.

The end-time circumcision of the heart bares the truth for examination,
                    bears the truth in righteousness,
                    bears the truth within the fear of God.

The end-time circumcision of the heart completes
                         at the end-point of decision-making,
                         at the end-point of readiness for the grave,
                         at the end-point just prior to transition's call.

The end-time circumcision of the heart informs the bride-to-be
                         of the need for preparation,
                         of the need for cleansing,
                         of the need for a final ridding of the grime—
                         that as found adhering from within mortality.

The end-time circumcision of the heart
         confirms entrance of the bride of Christ into the family of God;
         confirms entrance of the justified with the sanctified into the presence of God;
         confirms entrance of the committed with the redeemed as gathered in
                                   their gracefulness:
              so all who testify of following—
                   of being disciples of—
         The Living Loving God may be welcomed home amongst the stars of God."

My Content Study Aid

_____

_____

_____

_____

_____

_____

_____

The End-time Receptiveness of Man

"The end-time receptiveness of man to God
           is a measure of man's independence,
           is a measure of his needs not met,
           is a measure of his acknowledging the complexity
                of his surroundings—
                of how he sees himself relationally when
                        placed therein,
                of the reason for his being in experiencing life.

The end-time receptiveness of man is a function of achievement,
                is a function of the store of knowledge,
                is a function of the daily needs,
                is a function of the guarding of possessions,
                is a function of the evaluation of a threat.

The end-time receptiveness of man is dependent on his history with God:
                  of how he feels he has been treated by God,
                  of how he recalls his 'emergencies' in life,
                  of how he has been welcomed by the flock
                        of God,
                  of the level of his understanding of the
                      reality of God within his life.

The end-time receptiveness of man is coloured
           by experiences with those who profess to know their God,
           by his will to investigate without a pre-condition,
           by his interest in a subject which may impact in detail both a family and
                      each life,
           by the testimonies of relevance to his way of life which may enhance
                      his interest.

The end-time receptiveness of man is conditioned by his peers:
                in their regard for God,
                in their comments on God,
                in their perceived treatment by God.

The end-time receptiveness of man is highest at a turning point in life:
                when a decision affects a way of life,
                    affects a way of living,
                    affects the building of a family,
                    affects the present ethics in reaching out in
                      determining the relevance
                      of the morality of God.

- ANTHONY A EDDY (SCRIBE)

The end-time receptiveness of man sees him circling
in ever greater circles of despair,
in ever greater circles of silence,
in ever greater circles round a centre of denial.

The end-time receptiveness of man holds out his hand to see what comes his way,
holds close his hand empty of his gratitude,
holds up his hand as a signal of enough,
holds closed his hand with all that he can seize.

The end-time receptiveness of man sees him seeking a placeholder near to God,
sees him seeking as his wisdom increases
through experience,
sees him seeking as the years mount up upon the sand
within his hourglass,
sees him seeking as his health deteriorates,
sees him seeking as his time approaches,
sees him seeking as his values change within
his lifetime.

The end-time receptiveness of man knows the thrower of the boomerang,
knows to catch it with both hands,
knows its purpose and its trail within the sky.

The end-time receptiveness of man should leave a trail to God,
should leave a history of a narrowing search,
should mark a life with victory in acceptance of He
who stood beside him in all his days within mortality.

The end-time receptiveness of man should terminate in triumph,
should be present at the sealing of commitment,
should navigate a well-trodden pathway to the stars,
should be present at the accolade that only
God bestows,
should understand the impact of the gift of grace upon
each soul,
should express his undying gratitude for the changes
wrought within his spirit and his soul.

My Content Study Aid

_____

_____

_____

_____

Appendix

My End-time Calls for Man

"I,
    The Lord Jesus,
      am involved with man since his beginning—

                        in his time frame of the being of his presence,
                        in his shuttering against the storms and trials,
                        in his inoculations for good health,
                        in his preservation from demonic forces,
                        in his quest for wisdom,
                        in his accumulating knowledge.

I,
    The Lord Jesus,
      am the nurturer of creation,
        the instigator of the fathering of life,
        the springboard for existence,
        the bringer of awareness to the spirit of man,
        the participator in the progression of man towards his God,
        the prime mover in the exaltation of man as the end-time of preparation ends.

I,
    The Lord Jesus,
      am the epitome of completeness,
        the author of reconciliation,
        the architect of redemption,
        the offeror of salvation,
        the definer of morality,
        the good shepherd of His sheep.

I,
    The Lord Jesus,
      speak to man this day of his being in the end-time of his mortality,
            of his being at the cross-roads of existence,
            of his being subject to the tipping of the scales of
                            his freewill.

    For as the scales are tipped so the destiny is procured.
    For as the scales are tipped so the freewill of man decides.
    For as the scales are tipped so the existence in eternity becomes instated with a
                               dwelling place.

    For the scales of destiny are accurate and refined:
            verify the weight of sin,
            verify the presence of grace.

For the scales of destiny do not seesaw in indecision:
>> know the arguments of sin;
>> know the overwhelming bounty of grace.

So man pays the penalty of sin or receives the accolade due grace,
>> is destined for the depths of darkness or is uplifted to the light:
>> has his freewill demanding respect—
>>>> from the detailed record;
>> or has his freewill deserving honour—
>>>> born of righteous faith.

I,
> The Lord Jesus,
>> will greet all those awaiting Me,
>> will turn My back on those unknown and weighted down with sin.

The entry in The Lamb's Book of Life,
>> for each within mortality,
>>> is only valid,
>>> only remains on offer,
>>> only stands open for acceptance:
>>>> within a timeline shrinking fast,
>>>> within a timeline prior to My return,
>>>> within a timeline set for expiry on the use-by day.

The timeline as set for man has been determined by God.
The timeline as set for man is soon to reach its fullness.

The timeline as set for man is for his preparation,
>> is for his acquisition of wisdom born of God,
>> is for his enabling of a journey born of a freewill
>>>> commitment with honour to the fore."

Appreciatively received from The Lord for use in this, His book.
6.01— 7.14am Thursday 31st May 2012
Hamilton, NZ.

My Content Study Aid

_____

_____

_____

_____

_____

_____

- ANTHONY A EDDY (SCRIBE)

The End-time Vision From God

"I,

    The Lord Jesus,

        speak to My servant Anthony this day with a vision for The Earth,

                        with a vision for My advent,

                        with a vision all encompassing for the edifice

                                        of God.

I,

    The Lord Jesus,

        speak in affirmation,

        speak in testimony,

        speak in The Father's will of My servant Anthony's receiving of a vision,

                            declaring of a vision,

                            testifying of a vision.

For this vision comes from the throne room of God:

            is for this end-time of change,

            is for the tribulation of man,

            is for the presence of My bride,

            is for the politicians of The Earth,

            is for the prepared of God,

            is for the coming day of light,

            is for the governance of the Kingdom of God.

For this vision comes from The Trinity of Light:

            is for the advent of The Lord,

            is for the transitioning of the saints,

            is for the pouring out of the wrath of God,

            is for the rider on the white stallion,

            is for the witnessing of all upon The Earth,

            is for the fulfilment of My word,

            is for the coronation of the King of kings.

For this vision comes forth with My Spirit's seal:

            is for the multitudes as I have proclaimed,

            is for the sheep within the fold,

            is for the welcome to eternity,

            is for the curbing of the devil,

            is for the granting of grace to the end-time residue,

            is for the uplifting of My people,

            is for the sealing of My Bride.

Anthony has received a vision:

                      dictated straight from God,

complete within the books of God,
broadcast on the network of The Lord,
laid upon the table of The Lord as His end-time fare,
built upon completion for The Bride before The Altar.

Anthony has written down the fulness of the vision,
the intent of the vision,
the message of the vision:
so it may stand before the peoples of The Earth
without adulteration,
without exaggeration,
without the interference of man.

Anthony has scribed that which he has heard;
so it may herald truth with great validity,
so it may preserve the dictates of The Lord,
so it may bear witness to the nations of the
end-time on their lives.

Anthony has secured the vision in its scope,
the vision in its blessings,
the vision in its warnings,
the vision in its urgings,
the vision in its lambastings,
the vision in its magnificence of purpose.

Anthony has tied the end-time knot of God which holds the parcel of the record of
the promises for eternity,
the promises of eternity,
the promises for the committed to The Lord,
the promises which stand upon the rock,
the promises parcelled in the books of God,
the promises readied in the parcel for all
who will tie the knot which seals.

Anthony has a close relationship with God,
speaks the tongues of victory,
fulfils in honour and integrity the taskings of The Lord,
holds two way conversations,
knows the Spirit's presence in a temple,
carries the fear of God within his heart.

I,
The Lord Jesus,
speak to the world at large;
speak to the secrets closeted for shame;
speak to the rewards dressed for honour;
speak to the innocent imprisoned;

- ANTHONY A EDDY (SCRIBE)

speak to the guilty running free;
speak from a position of authority and knowledge—
     that man should understand all will be addressed,
               all will be exposed to light,
               all will see the gates of justice swing:
                         one way or the other;
speak what is necessary to accomplish:
          the will of God upon The Earth."

Also appreciatively received from The Lord for use in this, His book.
3.58— 4.26, 4.36— 5.26am Saturday 7th July 2012
Hamilton, NZ.

My Content Study Aid

_____

_____

_____

_____

_____

_____

_____

_____

_____

_____

_____

_____

_____

_____

_____

_____

_____

_____

_____

_____

_____

_____

The End-time Challenge of Mortality

"The covers of My End-time Psalms of God are vibrant and intriguing,
                                            are eye-catching and immersive,
                                            are readied for the seekers,
                                            are readied for the curious,
                                            are readied for My people,
                                            are readied for the multitudes:
                                                    as curiosity is aroused,
                                                    as a reaching hand moves—
                        from within the mortality of man into the eternity of God.

Expect the wonderful and the dramatic,
            the complex and the coloured,
            the attention-grabber and the head-liner,
            the prophecy-revealer and the mystery-unwinder.

Behold the arrival of the carefully prepared.
Behold the introduction of the end-time works of God.
Behold the commitment to the end-time Word of God.
Behold the alteration to a lifestyle with a change of destiny.
Behold the imprisoned in the drugdoms without bars.
Behold the lonely and the suffering where love is very rare.
Behold the sequences which everyone can master.

Behold the goal of God—
            to achieve the end-time company of man before man's hourglass becomes empty.

Reach out to those who cannot move,
                    who are stationary by cause,
                    who are set to wait,
                    who would fill the day where activity is low—
                                    but the intellect is high,
                    who would await the healing process where movement pauses—
                                    for the knitting of the bones,
                    who find themselves as housebound—
                                    with boredom as a foe to fight,
                    who sit and often wonder—
                            where is the God of love whereof the churches teach?

The willing God of eternity has a greeting hand in readiness,
                    has a place prepared,
                    has now released disclosures of that formerly hidden by
                                                            the grave.

- ANTHONY A EDDY (SCRIBE)

The God of the cross calls to man in triumph,
> has plans to share a victory,
> has scenes which stretch the incredulity of man.

The God of creation is active in His shepherding of man,
> is active with a searchlight beamed into the darkness,
> is active with His voice which calls the forlorn and hesitant unto a
>> golden future,
> is active with His servants who know the tune of salvation as
>> plays out—
>> among the kings and queens of God:
> with the princes and the princesses mimicking and mastering—
>> the challenges of the day encountered in their play.

The God of love,
> with knowledge intertwined with wisdom,
> issues His End-time word for the graduation of man,
>> for the advancement of man,
>> for the lettering of man,
>> for the wisdom of man,
>> for the gifts to man,
>> for grace within the time of man,
>> for the magnificence of eternity with the
>>> divine promises—
> all marked as reasons for embarking on a journey manned by God."

Appreciatively received from The Lord for use in this, His 4th book.
6.35 - 7.29pm Thursday 16th, 9.02 -9.14am Friday 17th March 2017
Hamilton, NZ

My Content Study Aid

_____

_____

_____

_____

_____

_____

_____

_____

_____

Journaling and Notes

Dedication

1 Peter 2:6-8 (NKJV)

A Chosen Stone and His Chosen People

6 Therefore it is also contained in the Scripture,

"Behold, I lay in Zion A chief cornerstone, elect, precious,
And he who believes on Him will by no means be put to shame."

7 Therefore, to you who believe, He is precious; but to those who are disobedient,

"The stone which the builders rejected Has become the chief cornerstone,"

8 and

"A stone of stumbling And a rock of offence."

They stumble, being disobedient to the word, to which they also were appointed.

Isaiah 28:16-19 (NKJV)

A Cornerstone in Zion

16 Therefore thus says the Lord GOD:

"Behold, I lay in Zion a stone for a foundation,
A tried stone, a precious cornerstone, a sure foundation;
Whoever believes will not act hastily.

17 Also I will make justice the measuring line,
And righteousness the plummet;
The hail will sweep away the refuge of lies,
And the waters will overflow the hiding place.

18 Your covenant with death will be annulled,
And your agreement with Sheol will not stand;
When the overflowing scourge passes through,
Then you will be trampled down by it.

19 As often as it goes out it will take you;
For morning by morning it will pass over,
And by day and by night;
It will be a terror just to understand the report."

Acknowledgements

This is the day that The Lord has made and we will rejoice and be glad in it. For mighty are His ways with man. Great is His foresight and integrity of purpose for man. Majestic and filled with great glory can be the destiny of man.

For as man develops in righteousness so the Lord applauds in favour, for as the sands of time near expiry so arrangements approach fulfilment, for as immortality arises over the horizon for each man so the time for a commitment is measured by the burning fuse.

May God our loving Father, Jesus Christ His Son, together with The Holy Spirit as our counsellor— bless and favour his family in all they do and bring to pass in the growth and development of His Kingdom here in New Zealand and around the world.

Marana tha— O Lord, come!

All donated funds received go in their entirety to
The Advent Charitable Trust, unless directed by a donor,
in order to further,
the scope and the objectives of this Charity's Christian Call
within The Kingdom of God.

The Banner of The Kingdom was first flown as a Flag at
10.30am on Monday, 1st September 2008
in Hamilton, New Zealand.

The Banner of The Kingdom was first flown as His Flag on His church
*in the village of **Burripalem***
near Tenali, Andhra Pradesh, in India,
on
Sunday, 31st July 2011
in unity with
Reaching Forward Ministries of Tenali, Andhra Pradesh, India.

- ANTHONY A EDDY (SCRIBE)

On a Personal Note

This book speaks of the welcome extended to man; the invitation like unto none other: the appeal to wisdom and to love— which sees the fullness fall for the end-time benefit of man.

For the chaos descends on the unreceptive soul, the turmoil on the soul destitute of faith, the wages of sin on the soul with the deafened and blinded spirit of man when captured by his soul.

For the season, when the promise of The Father* is served up to all who would uplift these offered gifts, is upon us— the season just prior to The Advent of The Lord.

*Ref.: The Books of Joel, 2:28–29, and of Acts, 2:17–21, The Bible, NKJV.

*I again have very real cause for gratitude in offering
the preparation of this, His fourth, book also into His care.*

*To our God of love, of justice, of redemption
who is very interested in all we do
and in our achieving our return home..
For He alone is worthy of the devotion of Man.*

Agapé,
Anthony,
His servant and His scribe.
Hamilton, New Zealand.

About the Scribe

Updated 9th April 2018

Anthony is 77, having been married to his wife, Adrienne, for 54 years. They have five married children: Carolyn, Alan, Marie, Emma and Sarah and thirteen grandchildren: Matthew & Ella; Phillipa & Jonathan; Jeremy, Ngaire & Trevor; Jake, Finn & Crystal; Bjorn, Greta & Minka.

Anthony was raised on a dairy farm in Springston, Canterbury, NZ in the 1940's. He graduated from Canterbury University, Christchurch, NZ with a B.Sc. in Chemistry and Mathematics in 1962. He was initially employed as an industrial chemist in flour milling and linear programming applications.

These used the first IBM 360 at the university for determining least cost stock food formulations and production parameters. Later he was involved in similar applications on the refining side of the oil industry in Britain, Australia and New Zealand. This was followed by sales and managerial experience in the chemical industry.

The family moved to a Bay of Plenty, NZ, town in 1976 when Anthony took up funeral directing, as a principal, expanding an initial sibling partnership until the close of the century. Anthony acquired practical experience in accounting, business management, and computer usage (early Apples - including the 'Lisa').

Upon retiring from active funeral directing in 2000 and selling his interests, he then commenced the promotion and the writing of funeral management software for the NZ funeral environment. Rewarded with national success, he has now also retired, in 2007, from that active management interest, living near some of his family in Hamilton NZ.

Anthony was brought up in the Methodism of his father until his mid-teens, his mother's side was Open Brethren. He is Christian in belief within an Apostolic Pentecostal framework of choice (since the 1990's) having been earlier in the Mormon church for several years. Thereafter he was in the Baptist denomination followed by finding a home within the Acts (Apostolic) church movement.

He and his wife, who has visited a number of Asian countries, have been to India in 2011, 2012, 2013, 2016, & 2018 on The Lord's tasks.

His forbears William Henry Eddy and Margaret Jane Eddy, emigrated to New Zealand from Gulval, Cornwall, England in 1878 on a sailing ship, with a very slow passage time of 79 days, and with their 3 month old infant child, Margaret Anne, dying "21st October 1878 from 'Congestion of the brain' on board the 'Marlborough' while en route to NZ".

The 'Marlborough' sailed London 19 Sep 1878, via Plymouth 26 Sep 1878, and arrived Lyttelton 14 Dec 1878 with 336 assisted immigrants. His grandfather, Alfred Charles Eddy, then but 3 years old, together with an older brother aged 4, obviously survived the trials of the sea voyage to become a part of a family with a further eleven New Zealand born siblings all living to maturity.

- ANTHONY A EDDY (SCRIBE)

Books 5 (3) & 6 (3) Reviews

Of Book 5— Three People are saying:

GOD Speaks in Letters of Eternity

1st Reviewer: AJE

Anthony Eddy has done it again; "GOD SPEAKS in Letters of Eternity", the fifth in the preacher's "God Speaks" series of poetry, is a masterpiece worthy of the centuries. It definitely deserves a place in any believer's ebook library.

Once again presented as a series of missives presented by the Lord to his fictional prophet, sharing the name of the author, this book focuses on the relationship of Jesus Christ to His people. I was particularly inspired by "The Inside of the Eyelids", the fifth of eighty-one poems, which shed light on God's plan through the use of a rarely-employed metaphor. Kudos, Eddy, for thinking outside the box.

A common feature of Eddy's writing is word repetition. For example, most of his poems begin with the same repeated word or phrase which is generally also the title of the poem, and I find that this works very well in a lyrical sense. This isn't always the case, of course, and those breaks from the pattern only serve to illuminate Eddy's unique and pleasing writing style.

In conclusion, I would gladly purchase "GOD SPEAKS in Letters of Eternity", and recommend it to anyone.

2nd Reviewer: EB

This book was much like reading a poem, or even parts of the bible itself. The book has an abundance of information about Jesus and the love he has to offer you. This is about God's purpose for us, not about man's purpose for man.

God speaks to us in many different ways and this book is one of those amazing and unique ways God shows his love. You will need patience and an open heart to read this book. It's so full of God's word, and amazing poetry that any religious, or even non religious people, will find the true beauty inside.

What an amazing and beautiful way for God to express his love for man. The poem like book also goes into detail of how Satan is full of evil and to ignore his cries and stay on God's side. This book even includes God's end of time prophecy. God has said in the bible that he will destroy the world and there is a poem that I felt shows the beauty in God cleansing the Earth of all evil. It's an amazing concept that God wants us to live in such harmony that he would go to such extents to make this possible for us.

Read this book to understand the message that Jesus is there for you to love him, and for him to love you back. His love is eternal and will never falter. He will forgive you and take the evil out of your soul and replace it with love.

I gladly give this book 5/5 because you can't dock points for Jesus.

3rd Reviewer: JD

I had read books by Mr. Eddy before and this one follows the pattern of the others. He is very consistent with his books and their contents. The sections have clear divisions, so the reader will not be lost even when they decide to stop reading and pick it up again at another time.

I always did enjoy how the author uses the poetry format for his books. It makes it extremely easy to read, and although it does contain a few things that are repeated constantly, the author does say this in the beginning, on the Index.

The book is definitely not for everybody, it takes a lot of time to go through it and as I had already mentioned, a fair bit of repetitiveness. But it is inspiring in the sense that every passage you read contains a great deal of positivity, and sometimes when you read things like this and it gets repeated, it ends up being instilled in your memory even better. Throughout the book, some readers might be confused by who the author means by "My People" and "My Spirit". If this turns out to be the case for you, just keep reading because eventually the understanding will come. The book talks about "eyelids" and "veins and arteries" of man in a spiritual sense, and it is important for the reader to understand that and grasp the proper context.

Overall the book is enjoyable to read, it is motivational and spiritually inspirational! Kudos once again to Mr. Eddy!

Of Book 6— Three People are saying:

GOD Speaks to His Bridal Presence

1st Reviewer: AJE

Yet another masterpiece in Anthony Eddy's "God Speaks..." series, "GOD SPEAKS to His Bridal Presence" is a collection of 115 religious poems that speak directly to the soul of a true believer. Like his other works, this book is presented in the format of Eddy's fictional avatar, a prophet, receiving missives from the Lord and recording them to spread to the world. My one complaint is that this fictional wrapping must be intuited from the text and is not explicitly shown, but any savvy reader will have no trouble deducing it. In the vein of his other works, "GOD SPEAKS to His Bridal Presence" carries a theme of fallen humanity's redemption from its sins via its trust in the Lord, and God's reciprocal love for and protection of His flock, us, His children. Frequently Eddy speaks of how Satan and his minions will be vanquished, bringing God's children into the light. Truly a must-have for any religious lover of lyrical prose.

- ANTHONY A EDDY (SCRIBE)

2nd Reviewer: DN

The poetry like format in this books makes it look much more appealing to people who are tired of reading massive brick-like books, which is a common attribute to religious books. If I were to go into a library or book store and get given two books -- one in this format and one in the 'normal' format -- I would definitely pick the one in this format, for it is much easier to digest.

However, like some have mentioned, the repetitiveness can get a bit, well, repetitive. It can be tiring to read a chapter which is basically the same thing throughout with a word change at the end of each sentence.

There are a lot of metaphors in this series, which do help to visualize God and the things Eddy is talking about in a quite pretty, and sometimes, if he's describing something horrific, a haunting way.

But there are also SO many words which the average person does not understand. This will either force that person to look the words up or to simply put it down. The majority might look it up but due to the constant use of these difficult words, they will eventually put it down. All I'm saying it maybe add in a few more common words.

Eddy does seem to understand Christianity well to have written a book about it, and even a series of books. They are much better than the common books in my opinion, but that may just be me and my way of not liking very long books!

Overall, absolutely no grammar or spelling mistakes. You just need to think about what I have mentioned and maybe change a few things around.

Good luck!

3rd Reviewer: SGS

GOD SPEAKS to His Bridal Presence by Anthony A. Eddy is a very interesting book; it's almost like the Bible. You may call it the author's version of The Bible. It is the best so far in the "God Speaks..." series by the author. The poetry like format in these books is the most appealing factor. It is, however, appealing to only those of us who are very strong believers. Most of the people don't have enough patience to sit through the book or the depth of philosophy to understand it. The writer is professing his beliefs through the book, hence, readers form a narrow group, so I'll have to be watchful while recommending it, since you can't tell everyone to go and check it out. The format is unique, and content is inspiring. It gives you superb insights, a new way to see things.

For a person who is religious, the book is awesome. But for a non believer or a not so strong believer, the book holds low charms. The book is almost a self help, and an inspiration, but from a religious standpoint.

I am giving a three star for this book. The message is very clear, and is inspiring, too. The book was very good but hard to understand. A commentary from the author is needed to understand it in the first go. But all in all, the book is a fine one and I'll definitely recommend it to my strongly religious group of friends. I'm sure they'll love it.

****